DREAMS and NIGHTMARES

Dreams
and Nightmares

A Book of Gestalt Therapy Sessions

Edited by
Jack Downing, M.D.
and Robert Marmorstein

A Publication of The Gestalt Journal Press

A Publication of The Gestalt Journal Press

Cover photo by Mimi Forsyth

Published by:

> The Gestalt Journal Press, Inc.
> A Division of:
> The Center for Gestalt Development, Inc.
> P. O. Box 278
> Gouldsboro ME 04607-0278
> U.S.A.

ISBN 978-0-939266-27-2

CONTENTS

Preface

In the past two years I have become enthusiastic about (1) Gestalt dream therapy, and (2) Jack Downing — not necessarily in that order; not necessarily in any order, but rather in conjunction with each other, for they have both become intertwined in my experience.

My exposure to Gestalt dream therapy did come first chronologically, and I reacted to it as a starving man would react to the discovery of food. After years of sifting through and examining various forms of therapy from Freudian-prone-on-the-couch to encounter-scream-at-your-neighbor, I found that Gestalt dream therapy was the quickest to reach one's emotional difficulties, and the most direct and successful in resolving those difficulties.

My subsequent enthusiasm for Jack Downing derived from my conviction that he is simply the very best Gestalt dream therapist I have seen in action. I first met Jack Downing at Esalen Institute, that beautiful blending of nature, intellect, and human awareness overlooking the Pacific Palisades at Big Sur, California, where I had gone to discover something of myself and to participate in dream therapy seminars. The room where our group, thirty-six of us, gathered to become acquainted with each other was filled with businessmen, schoolteachers, housewives, students, a couple of drifters, a couple of lawyers, a physician, a minister, an accountant, a drummer, a modern dancer, a beautician, and two or three psychologists. We had all been drawn there by the reputation of Esalen and Jack Downing.

When he finally arrived, my first reaction was disappointment. The famous Jack Downing looked to me like nothing more than another slightly tired businessman. He was neither very tall nor very short. He was not distinguished by a topping of wild hair nor was he dramatically bald. He was not appealingly fat or tragically skinny. His voice did not dominate the room. He seemed, in fact, like the rest of us, like any one of a hundred people you'd meet every week. He looked disappointingly normal.

It did not take me long, however, to recognize how very gifted he is at what he does. We began working on dreams, our own dreams, that very night, and the results were often very quick and very obvious. It did take me a bit longer to realize just why Jack Downing is so very good — what special talent he has that enables him to get inside other people, to understand, to actually become a part of other people's dreams.

The format that Downing uses to conduct his dream therapy is usually, wherever possible, a group setting. At Esalen our larger group was divided into three smaller groups; each smaller group of twelve stayed together for a week. The subject, the person whose dream is being worked on, sits alongside Downing in a chair Downing refers to as the "hot seat" and, guided by Downing, plays out the various roles of his or her dream, getting deeper and deeper into the subtleties of the dream and deeper and deeper into the center of himself or herself. Although Downing does not encourage much interaction between the subject and the rest of the group, he allows a certain amount of it if he feels it is honest and spontaneous. However, he is quick to cut it off if he feels it is diverting. The group setting serves a number of useful functions. It enables those who are watching to participate vicariously with the subject in the hot seat; to become aware of their own emotions and reactions to and interpretations of what is going on; and to explore the universality (or as Downing would prefer to say, the unity) of feelings in all of us. This is something you will probably discover for yourself as you read through the dream sessions recorded in this book. There is also a psychic energy in the group session that flows back and forth between the subject and the group. A sensitive group is aware of honest feelings and is quick to react to and reinforce these feelings. It is also aware of, and quick to react against, any phoniness.

What Jack Downing brings to these sessions is an unusual openness, a receptivity, an awareness of every breathing as well as nonbreathing thing around him. You could call it empathy, but it goes much deeper than empathy. I have watched him closely at work and have noticed that the rhythm of his breathing often matches that of the subject in the hot seat : Downing does not merely *understand* the subject, he *becomes* the subject. The objective *distance* that most therapists insist upon maintaining simply does not exist between Downing and his subject. When Downing works, he laughs, he cries, he gets angry, he gets bored, he gets excited, he gets involved, he gets turned on. He reacts immediately and actively to his subject. This is not easy, for it requires a willingness to remain open, a willingness to experience the pain as well as the joys of life spontaneously and intensely. It is a willingness I have found in very few therapists, in very few people. It is a part of Jack Downing.

I never think of Jack Downing as Joseph Jackson Downing, M.D., or even as Dr. Joseph Downing, for he seems beyond the confinements of formal titles. He has never allowed degrees and honors and the usual conventions to keep him from following a nonconventional course — a course of experimenting, innovating, experiencing, growing. Credentials mean little to him. He is more concerned about what a person is here and now, not what he was or what he did. But for those of us who need that sort of identification and orientation, Downing's credentials are impressive.

He graduated from medical school at twenty-one. After serving in the air force, he went on to the Menninger School of Psychiatry in Topeka, Kansas, where he wrote, directed, and produced the first of eight psychiatric films. After becoming a board-certified psychiatric specialist at the unusually early age of twenty-seven, his appetite for new ideas took him to Syracuse to learn about the then almost. specialty of social psychiatry. From 1953 to 1958 he pioneered in that field as research director of the Epidemiology Research Unit of the New York State Department of Mental Hygiene.

He then moved on to San Mateo, California, where for the next ten years he directed a program of county wide mental health services which under his direction grew from 15 to 150 employees and was subsequently praised by Dr. Maxwell Jones, the distinguished British social psychiatrist, as the best public mental health program in the world.

In 1961 he began experimenting with the clinical possibilities of LSD, becoming one of the first psychiatrists to recognize both the potential value and the potential danger of the drug. He published three papers on the results of his experiments and in 1961 wrote to all national food, drug, and psychiatric authorities calling for rigid controls, controls that were finally imposed five years later.

In 1965 he began his association with Fritz Perls, the founder of present-day Gestalt therapy. He became a companion and disciple of Perls, a relationship that lasted until the latter's recent death. With the help of Perls and other prominent Gestaltists, Downing founded the San Francisco Gestalt Therapy Institute and became its first president. He has conducted numerous Gestalt seminars, some devoted exclusively to the training of other professionals, at Esalen, California; the Bucks County Seminar in Pennsylvania; the Oklahoma City workshop; and elsewhere throughout the United States.

He has published over sixty scientific and professional papers, and one book, *A Comprehensive Community Mental Health Program: The San Mateo Experience.* In addition to his eight films, he has most recently written a television series of fifteen half-hour lectures on drug use and abuse.

In 1968, for those fortunate enough to catch him between activities, he opened an office for private practice in Palo Alto, California.

In 1970 Downing and his wife Leonne went to Arica, Chile, to study with Oscar Ichazo, who had developed from the ancient Oriental methods of Sufism a modern synthesis of physical and mental disciplines designed to raise human awareness to new heights. In 1971 both Jack and Leonne Downing, inspired by their year with Oscar Ichazo, helped to establish the first Arica School of America, in New York City. Jack was its first president.

Downing's continuing search for the inner potential, the core, the center of each human being is something like a religious quest. And, when you consider it, the religious aspect, the religious faith in the basic goodness and rightness of human awareness is essential to the search; or else, why is the search worth anything at all? Why should we struggle to break through to ourselves? Why should we undertake the tortuous road to the center of ourselves as human beings? Why should we learn to function as we were meant to function when the alternative, functioning like puppets of society, appears to be much easier? A personality course on how to win friends and be successful is so much simpler to follow than Jack Downing's road to self-discovery. But for those of us with faith, faith in the higher potential of human existence, faith in ourselves, there is no other road.

The words "here and now" and "discover" are important parts of Downing's work; and I am sure that he would advise that I stop telling you about him and allow you without any further delay to *discover* for yourself, *here* and *now* on the following pages. In doing so, you may discover something of yourself.

— *Robert Marmorstein*

Introduction

Dreams, what do they mean?

In dreams, the hardest aspect to accept is that every part of the dream is the dreamer: if I am driving along a dream highway, the car, the road, the passing automobiles, the distant mountains, the unseen dread, all are me. That's an important notion, a key to my place in the total pattern. In the dream as in life, I am the microcosm. I exist as a miniature replica, a scale model, of the universe, the macrocosm. I am the universe seeing itself through one particular distorting point. Beginning with me, my dream, I can reach out and stretch my arms to the entire universe, if I will but project fully. I am not the entire universe, to be sure; I am an exquisite, slightly self-aware, minuscule expression of the total. The car in my dream isn't my actual car, it is my impression, my memory trace of that automobile having attributes and opinions and attitudes coming from me, not the vehicle. My playing that little Gestalt game called projection separates that imaginary machine from me, puts that aspect of me outside, out there. I now can talk to it as separate from me. That car in my dream Gestalt is my car *for me,* as distinct from my car *as such* which is the particular machine parked in my driveway. So, what is involved in being able to carry out this apparent paradox is knowing that the dream figure is truly me, at the same time that I'm projecting out and pretending it-me is not me.

What can you do about understanding your dreams? In this book I suggest that you approach your dreams with the same interest, or the same disinterest, with which you treat yourself. For your dreams are you. They don't just *belong* to you — they *are* you.

This is a book for those of you who. are interested in yourselves, those of you with the curiosity and courage to journey inward into the undiscovered world of your inner self.

Each and every one of your dreams is an expression of an infinite number of associations, harmonies, conflicts, and contradictions that make up you. Each of your dreams may be used as a starting point on an endless road of self-awareness. The material in your dreams is like signposts along that road. Some of these signposts are bright; some are dim; others are completely dark and obscured. We try to illuminate them.

Each dream contains an *infinite* number of associations. How can that be? you ask. For some of your dreams are short, simple, one-dimensional, obvious. No such thing, I answer. You dream, for example, of a simple solitary shoe — nothing else. You ask yourself what could be infinite or endless about the interpretations of such a simple image. Let's find out.

Following the Gestalt law of dream formations, you would actually *become* the shoe. You, yourself, would live through the experience of being a shoe — desirable, comfortable, eventually worn-out, beat-up, cast off, abandoned, insignificant. The experience would be personal, exclusively yours, taking you through emotional twists and turns that may become frightening or exhilarating, lovely or ugly, that may even at times become boring and then suddenly ecstatic.

The seemingly limited material of that one dream could supply endless associations, endless opportunities for self-examination. You and I could work forever on that dream of a single old shoe, putting together the bits and pieces that are you. That is, *you* would work and I would merely assist. I would assist by prodding you, annoying you, frustrating you, forcing you deeper and deeper into the center of yourself. I would guide you, support you, and even become you.

Please accept that the Gestalt therapy I talk about here is *my* Gestalt, *my* thing. I do *my* thing, other therapists do *their* different things. And if you come to a workshop and find me doing the exact opposite of what I say here, all I can reply is "Yes, that was then, and now is now!"

For me, Gestalt therapy is releasing tied-up life, life that puts you in touch with all of your yous and gives a voice to the silent frustrated part of yourself. "Gestalt" is one of those lovely German words that can't be translated exactly. The meaning is something like "pattern" or "configuration." I don't dig either configuration or pattern much more than the word Gestalt, so the definition that I use is "unfinished business becoming finished; a pattern finally falling into place."

The old farmer who went to a circus and saw his first giraffe said, "Well, I see it, but I still say "there ain't no such animal." He refused to recognize a new Gestalt, the pattern we call "giraffe." A neurosis is a refusal to recognize a personal Gestalt or pattern; therefore it could be called unfinished business that refuses to get finished. The neurotic's life goes on repeating unfinished business like a cracked record.

The mental picture I have of my own neurosis is of a house cluttered with unfinished jigsaw puzzles. Unfinished puzzles on the table, puzzles on the floor, on the bed, in the john, with me walking around trying to step over this puzzle, around that puzzle, avoiding another one, and all the time I'm carrying around with me bits of one puzzle from one room trying to fit it together with bits of puzzle from another room. What a load! What confusion! What a waste of my energies!

If and when I finally get the puzzle finished, I can get the box out, put the puzzle in, and put it away, finished, complete. The cluttered space that the puzzle took up I can now *live* in. If I could finish all the puzzles, I'd have the whole house to live in. And what a relief that would be.

That's what we try to do in Gestalt therapy: help you finish the puzzles. Your dreams express Gestalts, usually many at one time.

The unfinished part shows up by the "splits," or "tensions," or "conflicts" in the dream. It is these conflicts we go after.

For example: You dream you are a child and want to eat some candy. Your mother won't let you. There's the conflict — you and mother, the child and the adult, unsatisfied desire and unsatisfactory reality. "You'll get cavities" your mother says. "What are cavities, Mommy?" "Cavities, are holes in your teeth that make you look ugly," your mother says. "And that cost a lot of money to get fixed," your father chimes in. "Who cares about stupid cavities?" you say. "I want candy. You don't love me." And here you are, right smack in the middle of the eternal problem, What does it mean? How do you work your way out of the problem? Only *you* know what your dreams mean; and only *you*, in your own way, can work your way out.

By you, I mean all of you, not just your brain, that egotistical, often selfish little guy who sits inside your skull peering out through your eyes and listening through your ears and officiously pressing buttons and switching dials. *All* of you means exactly that: your hands, your fingers, your feet, your toes, your skin, your stomach, your mouth, your tongue, your lips, your genitals, your fears, your feelings. Every single part of you has something to say about that piece of candy — and about Mommy. So until we've heard from all interested parties, until you've made contact with them and tried to resolve their differences, there is bound to be conflict within you — disabling, sometimes paralyzing conflict.

Once you are able to resolve a conflict, that particular Gestalt is completed, finished, in the box and out of the way. The energy that had been tied up in that conflict is now available to you and you are able to move on to new patterns, new Gestalts.

The more deeply you allow yourself to feel the experience and allow more parts of you, skin, muscle, guts, your entire self, actually to live through the experience, the deeper and more complete the learning. The Chinese knew this a long time ago. Children learning to read were given ideographs or letters made of candy and told to read them and eat them. That's learning the sweet way.

xvi

Some of you are probably thinking, but what about the *meaning* of dreams, the *symbolism* of dreams? You want to *understand*. In Gestalt therapy we don't worry about understanding, we concentrate on *experience*. The experience becomes *discovery* that is deeper and more complete than understanding because it is not limited to the level of intellectualization as so much therapy is. You can tell a child over and over again not to touch a hot stove and he'll nod. He understands. But only when and if he actually places a curious finger upon that hot stove does he discover what it's all about.

Did you ever try to explain an orgasm to someone who has never experienced one for himself? Sure he can "understand" intellectually, but one's "understanding" is a very limited and unsatisfactory substitute for the real thing itself, and only when we discover the thing itself can we really understand. So in Gestalt dream therapy we plunge as deeply as we can into the experience itself. And from this experience comes discovery and learning and growth and maturation — a maturation that enables us to live in this world as fully functioning human beings.

To return to the question of the so-called symbolism of dreams: If symbolism is what you're after, you don't have to bother with the trouble of working through your dreams. You don't have to bother with the often painful experience of making your dreams come alive. You don't need me, and you don't need this book. For a quarter you can buy one of those popular dream books from the corner newsstand. They're great for parlor games, if parlor games is what you're after. They may tell you that if you dream about water you're sexually frustrated, and if you dream about the color red you're very generous. Well, I wouldn't bet on it.

Dr. Sigmund Freud, who was somewhat partial to symbols himself, told us that a dream is a window into the subconscious. We think of it, in Gestalt therapy, more precisely as a window into the unintegrated — the unintegrated conflicts and torments and desires and joys of oneself. By inventing Gestalt therapy, Fritz Perls showed us how to climb in and out of that window. Sometimes I think of myself as a Peeping Tom who enjoys looking into your dream windows with you. I pay my dues by helping to straighten things out inside that window, by helping you to integrate yourself, by helping you to come alive.

How alive are *you*? In Gestalt therapy we do have a sort of measuring stick or scorecard to let us know where you're at, to give us an idea of how you're functioning. There are five personality layers that you must work through before you arrive at the truly authentic, alive, feeling, experiencing, expressive person that is you. These five personality layers were originally described by Fritz Perls.

The first layer's the cliche layer. We deal strictly in cliches-everyday, superficial, meaningless socializing. Good-morning-how-are-you-great-fine-nice-weather-well-be-seeing-you. No real contact. The chickenshit level, Fritz called it. No life at all.

The second layer is the synthetic or games-playing layer. Fritz referred to this as the Eric Berne or Sigmund Freud layer where we act out games and social roles. The very important person, the bully, the good boy, the nice little girl. Husband-wife game. Lover game. Boss game. Top dog-bottom dog game. President of these United States game. I play doctor, you play patient. That way I don't have to see you as a living, hurting person, and you don't have to see me as a fussy, tired, middle-aged man who makes mistakes and who hurts too. The danger is that after a while, there's no person there, only the game. Hollow men. No insides. No life. This is the unfeeling dangerous level. Gas chambers. ICBMs. My Lai. Law and order. I'm doing this for your own good. There is a little bit, a very little bit of contact at this layer, but a minimum of real-life. Mostly what Fritz called bullshit.

The third layer is the neurotic layer or impasse. Impasse means exactly what it sounds like. We cannot pass. We are stuck. We are phobic, lost, frozen in fear, uncertainty, and confusion. But here, for the first time, we are finally becoming aware of ourselves, of our own contradictions and distortions. We do not know how to deal with them yet so we remain rooted in the middle of the mess, existing in sort of an antiexistence, an avoidance of real anger, real love, real tears, real happiness. Our usual defenses, our games and cliches, no longer work, and we are now facing ourselves as human but perplexed beings. But we do not know how to proceed.

The fourth layer is the implosive or death layer. This is the logical extension of the third layer. The fear of the impasse is now fully felt. *All* defenses have been abandoned and we are in touch with the dead center, the core of our neurosis. Our life forces, our needs and emotions that we had so long denied, are now being felt and are striving to be dealt with. For the moment, though, all this energy is being forced inside and held there rigidly. We feel contracted, compressed, withdrawn deep into a motionless center of ourselves, a feeling often described as deathlike.

And then we come to the most awesome transition of all.

The fifth layer is the explosive or life layer. The energy held deep inside ourselves begins moving. The implosion becomes explosion. Explosion — energy going out, free. We have made contact with our real selves, the authentic within us. We have made contact with life. There are, according to Fritz, four basic kinds of explosion: grief, anger, orgasm, and joy. To these four I would add a fifth — ecstasy. We now have complete freedom to feel, to experience, to be responsible. To be able to respond is to be response-able. Able to respond to love, to pain, to work, to play; responding without turning off, without game playing. Alive with free energy. Free from organization, social conventions, the insurance premiums, the installment payments. Free to laugh and free to cry. Free to soar and free to fall. Free to succeed and free to fail. Free to love and free to lose.

Few if any of us exist completely in only one of the above layers. Most of us move from one to the other, sometimes swiftly, sometimes advancing to one layer then sliding back to another. Some of us never reach the fifth layer, never really allow ourselves to touch our authentic selves. Some of us never get beyond the second layer.

As you read the dreams on the following pages you will find examples of people moving into each of the five layers. See if you can determine where each one is at any given moment. See if you can distinguish authenticity from bullshit, life from lifelessness. See if you can determine where *you* are.

We were taught, as we grew up, to think there are two faucets to life: one marked "Pleasure" and one marked "Pain." Now we have finally discovered there is but one faucet, and it is marked "Awareness." If we turn off the faucet we think is marked "Pain," we're turning off all awareness. We feel neither pain nor pleasure. We feel nothing. We are empty, dead.

The purpose in Gestalt therapy is to keep that awareness faucet flowing, full and clean, and to unclog it if it's clogged. In dream therapy I encourage you into role-playing, sometimes painful role-playing, in order to get you in touch with your essence, in order to unclog the true existence of the person you are — *here and now.*

Although these pages are my own personal Gestalt there is nothing that is purely original and exclusively Jack Downing. Fritz Perls did it all first. He's the founding father of Gestalt — Big Daddy. My dreamy friends dreamed the dreams and worked out their own Gestalts in the workshops. Sony made the tape recorder. My nephew Jack copied the tapes and my friend Lyn typed them. Bob Marmorstein suggested the idea in the first place, patiently encouraged me, and then edited out as much of my bullshit as he dared. I just sit around listening and pass out Kleenex. I also kibitz a little and tell jokes. Some Gestalters like Jim Simkin are famous for their sharp, funny stories. My groups get stuck with my corny stories. But then, Jim's Jewish and I'm from Oklahoma.

OK, enough. End of the beginning. Let's go to work! The hot seat is empty. Who has a dream to work on?

— *Jack Downing, M.D.*

xx

1

The Hermaphrodite and the Dead Man

This is the morning of the last day at the Bucks County Seminar Center. This is a "professional workshop." What professions are represented I never do quite find out. I become so involved in what people are now that their pasts touch me very little. When I began doing workshops a heavy feeling of I-Am-Responsible kept me afraid of failing if some professor this or psychoanalyst that was present. "I" was phobic so "I" avoided knowing anything about the group. Eventually I realized my only responsibility is to be aware of my own total present reaction to the person and to the group. My entire being is now centered in the one person working with me. If my breathing is tight his breathing draws my attention. Should I find my left hand tightly gripping, holding on, a statement is being made about him. I'm in full contact, no longer scared or phobic.

Dreamer Jim is an unusually appealing young man. Handsome, well-sculptured features, long clean hair, glossy brown and curled in natural ringlets standing boldly out from his head. His youthful chin,

<1>

rakish moustache, and round steel-rimmed glasses complete the portrait of a typical trendy young man.

This being a sunshine-glorified autumn morning, the old ax-cut barn timbers enclose us with a particular private focus. Somehow each person lounging on the oriental carpets is linked into Jim and me, amplifying our energy with their own.

Jim's soft, resonant voice is supercool, with little emotion, a bit as though amused by me, himself, the whole situation. I don't know what to expect, but then, I rarely do.

JIM. I dreamed this last night. First part I don't remember very well. Somebody pisses off about something and I wind up murdering him. (*voice gets stronger but also sounds weary*) There is this folder, there's a folder in the room with some pictures I'd looked at, and after I left the room to go away, I remembered and really worry about getting caught by the authorities. I remember that my fingerprints are all over. And I say, "God, I've got to go back and get those pictures with my fingerprints because I'd looked at them." I can't remember what the pictures were So I go back and it's a boarding house. There's these two people I know. I meet them and they've already taken the pictures away. I try to find the pictures without letting them know about it, but I can't find the pictures and then the scene switches.

There's this girl, young woman that I'm with, who has, she doesn't have any top on, she has medium sized breasts, and a pair of underpants. We wind up going to bed and I take off her underpants. I find she has a penis, which she seems a little embarrassed about. But then I look further and find she *does* have a vagina, only it's small. I feel her up and find it's only an inch long. But my discovering this makes her very happy. Like she wasn't sure of it herself. And . . . that's it.

This dream is rich in potential — the split between Jim's languid boredom and the dream's violence, his sexual surface masculinity and

<2>

the dream's confused female-male. Right now I'm aware of his statue-like immobility as he sits. I feel the same binding constraint in my own chest. There is a breathlessness, as though my air goes only into the surface of the lungs, not filling or satisfying me.

JACK. All right ... what are you experiencing now?

JIM. I feel a lot of tension in my chest, in my arms, and a slight nausea in my gut! And my jaw is trembling slightly.

His voice is even more monotonous and unfeeling than before. He is clamping down to keep control. At this point I have a choice — stay with the physical experience, always a safe bet, and go into the dream content.

JACK. Talk to the hermaphrodite.

Taking dream content rather than Now physical experience is like the quarterback's choice between running and passing, between grinding out sure yardage or going for the big gain. I make the play for the big gain. I choose to explore the personality conflict in Jim, in which he is at war with himself, and bring that split out in the open so that it may be over and done with. Jim's surface sex is male, his dream self bisexual. I direct him to *project*, but outside himself, the bisexual dream self. The dream has provided the split, so Jim can imagine the woman-man sitting in a chair placed opposite him. He can now become involved with his own autonomous fantasy. As an unconscious fantasy the image was not approachable but was powerful in influencing Jim nonetheless. Now as a conscious projection she-he can be dealt with.

JIM. (*talking to a stool placed two feet in front of him*) You know, I'd really like to go to bed with you but you're too small. I'm not

<3>

going to fit. That penis of yours makes me uncomfortable, it's a little bit strange . . .

Jim is less discouraged by his anatomical discovery than I would be. People in their twenties today have fewer sexual hang-ups than we middle-aged types did at twenty.

JIM as hermaphrodite. (*Jim moves to stool and talks to the chair. His voice is higher*) I'm disappointed you can't screw me; I'm kind of embarrassed about having a penis like that.

JIM. You need a bigger vagina and no penis. I've already got a penis, I don't know what I would want with yours . . . (*he looks towards me*) I got a brief image of my mother again. (*both hands are clenching fiercely*)

JACK. What are your hands doing?

JIM. (*surprised, totally unaware of his hands*) Hands . . . ?

JACK. Give your hands a voice. Let your hands talk.

Feeling blocks are either complete or partial. A total block wipes out everything. Jim has a partial block. All body actions and feelings are here, only he can't let himself notice what is happening. I act as his notice.

JIM as hands. We want to go out, to go out to her . . . and strangle her and SHUT HER UP!!! (*screaming and clawing*) Stop her from TALKING! Mom . . . (*near crying and trembling*) *shut up*!

Emotion, anger, killer rage for the first time. He sits forward in his chair, a teeth-exposing snarl as his glasses fall from one ear. His voice is like ice breaking up on a frozen river. I put a thick padded club between his clenched hands. He squeezes. The blood swells in his face.

<4>

SHUT UP SHUT UP! GOD DAMN YOU!! SHUT UP!. . . You WILL NOT CALL ME THAT AGAIN. AHHHGGG . . . (*hands clenched on an imaginary throat, he is crumpled on the floor, against the stool which he has crushed throwing himself from the chair. Hands choking the imaginary throat, his breath is fast and shallow*)

JIM. (*suddenly he picks himself up, immediately becoming the cool young man again*) You'll have to get a stronger stool . . .

JACK. Notice now, you are right back in your control.

JIM. She's standing there with a . . .

JACK. You're either tightly controlled or destructive, there's no in-between for you.

JIM. (*sighs — weary*) A big head and a little body, standing there, knee high and smiling . . .

JACK. Anybody you know?

Here I'm taking a chance again. Jim broke through to real feelings for a moment. His level 2, game-playing behavior exploded into level 5, life-expressing anger. Then, like one of those self-sealing automobile tires, he is right back game-playing the cool, unemotional young man again. This is the stuff choir boy murderers are made of, sweet, gentle, good boys — then pow! My alternatives: quit now, accepting the dent Jim has made in his defenses as enough, or go ahead for more progress and risk using up that real life energy in words, bullshit, phoniness, game playing.

JIM. Yeah, it's my Mom, and Dad is right beside her.

JACK. They're down there, like dolls? OK, be your parents.

JIM as mother. (*voice muffled, rapid, distant, high*) Son, we don't know how to talk to you, you're going to have to do it yourself.

<5>

JIM as father. (*voice clearer, lower*) You can talk with our heads. (*stops; clears throat painfully*)

JACK. What's with your throat?

JIM. It's hoarse with all that shouting — it's also tense.

JACK. Let your jaw hang loose.

JIM as father. We talk with our heads, not with our bodies.

JIM as mother. Your father's like that, I'm not . . . (*pause*)

JACK. Are you going to let your father speak?

JIM as father. C'mon Mary, you don't know what you're talking about . . . All you ever do is withdraw from the conversation when it gets too hot for you. We've been through this a lot of times before and I'm not going to discuss it anymore. I'm leaving!

JIM as mother. Son, for Christ's sake, don't turn out like your father! Face the world! Don't keep running away from it with your head in the clouds!

JIM. (*highly controlled voice*) Wellll Mommmm, what you say is *right*, but your method of delivery is *so* loud . . .

JACK. Can you hear the superior tone, the contemptuous tone in your voice?

JIM. There's a sneering quality.

JACK. All right, tell her what you're doing: "I'm *sneering* at you."

Words lie ("Mom what you say is right . . . "), however, the tone of voice seldom lies. Jim game plays — level 2 — by using the socially approved words and at the same time saying the opposite by his tone. I bring Jim closer to his fear — level 4 — by joining words to voice tone. Now at least he is neurotic — level 3 — no longer pure game-playing bullshit.

<6>

JIM. Mom — I'm sneeeerrrinng (*exaggerated phony tone*) at you. I'm still trying to get back at you. I'm still the little boy. I can't come out directly and tell you.

JACK. (*interrupting*) You're making a speech.

JIM. (*with more feeling*) Sometimes Mom, you give me a pain in the head — (*pauses and voice changes to genuine surprise*) Sometimes you're great.

JACK. Try this for size: "I have to be grown up because *you're* such a child!"

My putting words in Jim's mouth is safer than it seems. Jim can accept or reject from his own experience. Often as not, the thought will be rejected, reworked, or put in the opposite.

JIM. (*speaking in voice of his mother*) I have to be grown up because you're such a child.

JACK. How does that feel?

JIM. Feels right . . . I want to speak to you as one equal to another Mom, I really do. But (*softly*) I never seem to do that, I never seem to, you or anybody else. A petulant child. An all-encompassing mother . . .

JACK. You have this rhythm, da dah da dah da dum, sling away at the end.

JIM. Da dah da dah da dum. I *am* so *pa*-tient *with you*-u-u. Mom, that keeps our game going . . . I've run out of words.

JACK. (*amused*) That's a pity.

JIM. Mom, you look old (*softly, as though talking to himself*) . . . I'm stuck (*decisively*) . . . That's it! . . .

JACK. That's what?

JIM. That's all —

JACK. That's what?

<7>

I'm asking Jim to be aware of the "it" in "That's it." The impersonal pronoun "it" conceals "me," as "That's me." We hide our own feelings and involvement by being impersonal saying, "it."

JIM. I can't go any further.

Jim has now become bottled up in level 3, the impasse zone. My purpose is for him to become aware.

JACK. You said "That's it."
JIM. I'm stuck.

This "stupidity" is characteristic of the impasse situation. I'm blocked, I can't think, understand, even hear.

JACK. Substitute "me" for "it."
JIM. That's me. (*clears throat*)
JACK. Yes or no?
JIM. It's ridiculous, but it's yes . . .

Again we could stop here. Jim has made a partial closure of the Mom impasse. "Mom, you look old" shows he has begun to see her in the Now, not in those past caricatures of the big-headed doll or the all-encompassing mother. I'm not satisfied; I smell the possibility of a more complete, satisfying closure. This entire dream work has felt flimsy, wordy, head-trip intellectual since Jim's explosion against his mother. Through the dead crust of his conventional, socially-approved self-control erupts a glowing fragment of genuine life. And then this is gone. For a few minutes Jim is alive, *does* break through the level where opposing energies deadlock into stalemate and suck up great amounts if his life energy, leaving him flat, dull, lifeless. I'm

<8>

eager to see him burn with the radiant fire of life for more than a few moments. I take another chance.

JACK. Return to the dream. An encounter between the murdered man of the first part of the dream, and the hermaphrodite of the second part.

I'm looking for an opening. An encounter between two main parts of the dream is obvious. Both hopeful and bored, I play long odds. The group watching us is yawning, shifting in their places. They too are bored, are losing their involvement with Jim and with me. A fairly sure symptom that I'm not succeeding in connecting Jim to his here-and-now self.

JIM. Okay. Hermaphrodite in this chair, murdered man there.

JIM as hermaphrodite. (*voice feminine, scornful, upper register*) You scare me, you're such a coarse, insensitive, gross slob.

JIM as murdered man (*voice deep, hoarse, masculine*) Well, hell, baby, that's your hang-up.

JIM as hermaphrodite. I want to *do* something, but ... I feel very uncomfortable. I can reach out and touch you but at the same time I'm repulsed by you.

JIM as murdered man. Tough. I mean when I want something I go out and get it. *I* don't have indecision. If what I want isn't what you like, that's *your* problem, not mine ... I don't really feel concerned about you. Your being uptight bothers me, gets on my nerves. Your having a penis gets on my nerves, women shouldn't have penises. Women should be women and men should be men. What the hell kind of game are you playing, anyway?

Jim has the great American sexual image. Men are men and carry big guns — penises; women are women and are submissive and look

<9>

pretty. Anyone who doesn't fit this black and white picture must be a pervert. Sadly enough for Jim — and for 100 million other American men — he knows he doesn't quite fit the socially certified image. Therefore, what does that make him?

JIM as hermaphrodite. I don't know. I was just born this way. (*defensively*) I can't help it if I have a penis! I have a vagina too but it's too small to be of much use. Do you have a penis?

JIM as murdered man. Oh what the hell do you mean! Of course I have a penis. All men got penises. Now that's strange, I got one, and I don't! It's there and it isn't. You know, I think you got the other half. That don't feel right. I want it *all*. You got to give it back, you got to give it to me . . . (*voice weaker, lacks conviction*)

The distance between these two is closing, they are becoming one psychic image.

JIM as hermaphrodite. Well, how can I give it to you? It's attached to me — I can't just cut it off! . . .

JIM as murdered man. Why *not*! You don't need it, just makes you embarrassed . . .

JIM. (*pauses, looks confused*) I'm losing my maneuverability between . . .

JACK. What's happening?

JIM. I feel like ah, ah, mixing. The more I move between one and the other, the less distinct each one is becoming.

A beautiful example of the split being closed by the open face-to-face encounter between the opposites, the effeminate uncertain hermaphrodite and the rough masculine murdered man.

<10>

JACK. OK. (*long pause*) Sit back over here next to me. (*Jim moves to opposite chair*) Is there anybody in that chair now?

JIM. Seems to be just a vague foggy form.

JACK. All right — can you absorb that fog into you?

JIM. (*concentrates for several minutes*) Now *I* feel foggy, it's gone now. (*voice solid, resonant*)

JACK. You feel foggy — how do your genitals feel?

JIM. They feel somehow more solid than the rest of me.

JACK. OK. That's all right, let's stop here.

This technique completes taking the projected part of Jim back into his aware, integrated self. The voice change from the high effeminate hermaphrodite and the growly deep murdered man to the mid-range, solid, resonant *new* personal tone of Jim tells me we were successful. Jim has done the important gestalt work in completing his sexual identity. The rest of the work will take place by natural growth. People sure in their own sexual identities are pleasantly aware of their genitals. For a man this means the testicles as well as the penis; for a woman the vulva and vagina and often the uterus and ovaries too. Jim's sexual identity is more solid at this moment than his entire self.

REFLECTIONS ON THE DREAMWORK

How has this closure of the split between the feminine and the masculine come about? Jim is caught in a very common conflict: his sexuality, which basically is entirely one, is split into two under the force of social attitudes and expectations. The picture he gets from childhood is that he must be either rough, unfeeling and thus masculine, or he will be considered passive, effeminate, and weak. You recognize this commonplace either-man-or-woman split as the

<11>

universal all-purpose American Sexual Identity Dilemma. In our immature society, television, schools, movies, magazines, sports, advertisements, nearly all mass information presents the ideal man as rough, two-gun John Waynes and women ideally as the sexually seductive, big-titted, wide-hipped Raquel Welch. These ideal images are caricatures of course, but caricatures that are held as the "normal" model by the Establishment.

The power of these images is shown by their presence in Jim's dream in undisguised form. Through the death of the fearful over-whelming masculine (father) image and coming to terms with the feminine (mother), the opportunity for blending the two separate aspects into one occurs. Sexually Jim should not have to play games. He is what he is in the Now, tender, receptive, rough, whatever, without following the impersonal phony media society laid on him.

Depending on many factors, a man may be both tender and dominant, a woman forceful and receptive, and neither need have any concern over whether they are "man" enough or "woman" enough. They both are persons, their own persons, and that is all there is or can be. In every life situation the integrated, awake person finds infinite variety, just because *he* is not limited to a few old mechanical dusty roles, pushbutton responses like Mommie's boy, good guy, hard guy, slick businessman, femme fatale, big sister, and so on.

Using the technique of the split and projecting that split image into an encounter, these shadow figures are dragged out in the open and reveal their flimsiness. The endless struggles between seemingly irreconcilable opposites are finally experienced as just cartoon Maggie and Jiggs, Tom and Jerry battles. The little child is terrified by quarrels between parents and hears the gods warring in high Heaven; the grown-up is bored and repulsed by the same unending squabbles and says, "Cut it out Dad and Mom, you're acting like a couple of senile brats!"

Jim hears with his own ears this difference and his healthy growing self responds. No amount of *telling* by me can do this. Jim must find his own way. I follow him, point by point, staying in my own

<12>

center of self-awareness in order not to have *my* problems interfere with *Jim's* work. Jim is on the same path I am on. He is changing from childhood dependence and the ordinary two-way splits of the immature personality to adult integration and a sound unified self. If he continues on this path he will become aware of the greater unity beyond one person, the unity of Love shared with other living creatures.

Going back to the dreamwork, Jim has closed one gap and his life energy has gone from a minus drain to a plus surplus in the sexual area. Instead of wasting energy fighting himself, he gains energy as the smooth flow of his sexual potency becomes one powerful stream instead of two opposing flows. This is level 5, the life layer.

Jim has gone partially through (has actually started) the most primitive of human processes — chewing and swallowing. He is learning to digest properly his experiences, his mental images, the same way the physically healthy learn to digest their food. Proper digestion consists of chewing, swallowing, coughing up or discarding unnecessary or indigestible portions, and assimilating the valuable. When I eat a beefsteak I want the energy and the life material of the meat to become Jack, not Jack to become the beefsteak. When I get opinions and attitudes and habits from close contact with someone, dear old Dad say, I want those habits and opinions and attitudes to give life, individuality, energy, and personality to Jack, but not for Jack to become a reasonable facsimile of dear old Dad.

Will this experience, this partial closure of the Dad-Mom, John Wayne-Raquel Welch, masculine-feminine, active-passive, fucker-fuckee, top dog-bottom dog gestalt make Jim a new and better man? Yes. How new and how better? I can't say. This sexual identity gestalt is powerful. Jim will experience himself as different in a seemingly different world. He is still partially asleep and beginning to suspect he is asleep. Some day soon he may decide he would like to wake up completely.

<13>

2

The Gallant State Trooper

This is another dream from the Bucks County Seminar Center. As you've gathered, I'm enthusiastic about Bucks County. Sadly, it's now closed. This particular morning, first thing, just as the barn furnace rattles and bangs into action, a friendly, quiet, young schoolteacher asks if she can work. I reply ungraciously, "I'm not going to give you permission." She figures out that I mean, "You must decide," gives herself permission, and sits down on the hot seat. A small point, you say? However, this establishes who is doing what and for whom. I, Jack, refuse to take responsibility for you, Jean. [*]

JEAN. I had a dream last night that I want to work on.

---

* To my surprise, when she read the dream, Jean told me that her dream about the state trooper had been fused with another dream. However, the resultant synthesis makes the basic bioenergetic point very well.

<15>

JACK. Fine, hold on a minute. (*starts tape recorder*) OK, tell it in the Now, first person, present tense. I am . . .

JEAN. (*voice firm and soft*) I am in a car with a girlfriend. She is driving. She has violated some traffic rule and a state trooper saw us. And as she stops I say, "You get into the passenger seat and I'll get in the driver's seat." I don't know why I did that. I felt that I had to do it. The state trooper was coming toward the car. I asked for her driver's license in case he has seen us switch. Then I could show him her driver's license, but she said, "Oh, my license expired last year." So the state trooper came over. He didn't say anything about the switch. He said he'd have to take us in. So we followed him into this building, which was the police station. There was this long table with chairs on either side. On one side there were policemen, on the other, civilians. The were talking back and forth, each with a pile of papers between them. At the end of the table was a place for one more policeman and I thought that's where we're going to go. But instead he took us — this state trooper was tall and had boots and the whole bit — he took us into this panel office with a shiny desk and a red carpet and proceeded to seduce both of us. And I thought, I knew that was going to happen. I didn't care, you know. Better than being arrested, and so...

GROUP. (*laughter and a voice says*) Just relax . . .

JEAN. (*smiling shyly*) That's the end of the dream.

JACK. What aspect of the dream interests you particularly? (*I see no obvious split so I throw the ball back to Jean*)

JEAN. Why I switched seats with my girlfriend. I don't understand that.

JACK. (*her response suggests a split with her girlfriend. Still, that doesn't feel right to me, so I stall*) All right . . . uh . . .

JEAN. (*half laughing*) I feel nervous.

<16>

JACK. (*here it is. A more definite clue at the body physical energy level. For "nervous" I translate "excited."*) Where do you feel nervous?

JEAN. In my legs. (*a trembling is visible along the inside of her thighs. She looks down at them as though the trembling is not connected to herself*)

JACK. Stay with your nervousness, just let it ... exaggerate the trembling ... (*pause*) What is happening now?

Jean's dream, with its open sexual theme, is proceeding to work itself out at the body energy or "bioenergetic" level. Words are not important here, only the direct physical experience. My directions are intended to guide Jean in releasing her damed-up energies.

JEAN. (*softly*) It's stopped. Now it's starting again. I have palpitations.

Her face is blushing. There is a trembling of her thighs and pelvic area accompanied by an irregular tightening and relaxing of her breathing. I recognize the gestalt of orgasm; the sensation of warmth and swelling as blood fills Jean's genitals. All this seems to be coming as a surprise to Jean. She apparently has not let herself be aware of her unsatisfied sexual needs.

JACK. What are you feeling in your genitals?

JEAN. Warm ...

JACK. All right, be aware of that warmth. (*pause; Jean is looking down*) I want you to put the state trooper in the other chair and ask him if he knows you had switched seats.

JEAN. (*laughing softly*) I have no idea where this is going to go and it's so funny.

JACK. Well, tell that to the state trooper.

<17>

JEAN. I don't have any idea why you're very imposing. And handsome. And it's warm. (*group laughter*)

The group and I are feeling Jean's sexual vibrations very strongly. We're starting to be turned on. Jean is both a little embarrassed and encouraged that everyone is laughing in mixed excitement and pleasure.

JACK. Now be the state trooper.

JEAN as state trooper. (*in deeper falsetto voice*) I know it. (*more laughter*)

JACK. How do you feel as the state trooper?

JEAN as state trooper. Very self-assured and confident. (*voice louder and firm*) Towering . . .

JACK. What's happening?

JEAN. Palpitations again.

JACK. All right, come back here to your own seat and say to the state trooper, "You excite me."

JEAN (*moves to first chair, breathlessly*) You excite me.

JACK. Ask, "Do you know I traded seats with Mary?"

JEAN. Do you know I traded seats with Mary?

JEAN as state trooper. Doesn't seem to be important whether I know it or not . . . I don't know what to say to you.

JACK. What's happening?

The Jean-trooper split is not a clear one. Jean has to be returned over and over again, a clear sign that it is not in the right direction. In fact, Jean's performance as the trooper tells me that words aren't the best way for making a breakthrough from her impasse into level 4, the implosive level, and hopefully even further, into the explosive

<18>

layer. I'm confirmed in my instinct to move her into the bioenergetic area, to help her melt her frozen sexual energy. Physical expression seems to be the only way through for her. Words will only interfere.

JEAN. (*very confident*) I'm not afraid of him!

JACK. Tell that to him.

JEAN. (*with assurance*) I'm not afraid of you.

JEAN as state trooper. You know I'm not going to hurt you, we're just going to have fun together. No trouble with the law.

Now the split becomes clearer. The trooper is Jean's masculine side of course. Jean has been afraid of her own active maleness and, therefore, of strongly masculine men. Her fear is covered up by the "no's" of society: "Sex is dirty, sex is forbidden, sex is against the law." And here her male side solves the problem. He *is* the law.

JEAN. I feel silly.

JACK. Do you like feeling silly?

JEAN. My legs are beginning to shake again.

JACK. Lie down on the floor. (*general laughter from group*) Or perhaps you'd rather not?

I have decided to use a bioenergetic exercise to release the energy held back in her thigh, belly, and pelvic muscles. As Jean lies on her back, I tell her to bend her knees so that her heels are close to her bottom, and then lift her bottom off the floor an inch or so. This puts a strain on all these muscles which causes them to begin to vibrate strongly after a few minutes.

I become conscious of the group's laughter and suddenly realize that it is directed at me because I am obviously and visibly turned on by the activity on the floor. I become aware of my own voice, which I had not permitted myself to hear before, and realize that my

<19>

directions to Jean are being given in a sexually seductive manner. I am embarrassed by this for I still retain my share of hang-ups, one of them being a twinge of guilt at not maintaining the traditional medical taboo against displaying real feeling — especially sexual — toward a patient. To cover my embarrassment, I adopt my most professional voice — bland and neutral — and ask Jean's permission to continue. She's already on the floor and not the slightest concerned about my professional or nonprofessional posture. She doesn't even bother to answer. I place a cushion under her head.

JACK. Bring your knees up comfortably. Now start belly breathing, not with your chest . . . That's good. (*Jean closes her eyes as she relaxes into belly breathing. I see that she is held in by her tight blue jeans*) Undo your waistband and unzip your fly to give more room.

Her hands unclasp the wide belt buckle, unfasten the waist band and unzip the jeans. Breathing becomes deeper and slower, moving down into her lower belly. Still, there is some sense of tightness in her breathing.

JACK. Allow each breath to go deeper until you feel the breathing all through your genitals.

Gradually I note a sense of expansion in Jean's pelvis. Her muscles are beginning to relax and stretch the way nature intended. Her lifelong habit of tightness, of pulling in and holding back, of saying, "Stay away; keep out," is giving way to a deep natural flow of breath. Good breathing should be like the tide moving in and out of the river's mouth by natural forces, flooding, nourishing, and cleansing the estuaries of the body. Jean comes to life. Her slender torso stretches, lengthens with each breath. Her breathing becomes increasingly deeper and fuller. Her knees, which were touching each other, holding tightly, protectively to each other, now slowly relax

<20>

and tilt outward. Her face softens, is younger. A little trembling is seen through her pullover sweater, just above her belly button.

JACK. (*kneeling beside her*) Just lift your rear a little higher off the floor. Keep on belly breathing.

Jean now supports her weight on her shoulders and heels, which are about six inches from her bottom. The muscles in her thighs tremble under the strain, then the trembling extends up into her belly.

JACK. Good! Exaggerate that trembling!

Jean vibrates most strongly. She moves her pelvis back and forth rhythmically. There is a crescendo of movement — open, direct fucking movement climaxed by a deep pelvic thrust downward and forward with a deep sigh. A ripple of muscle movement spreads down from her chest into her thighs, like a line drawn down her body. Jean opens her eyes and smiles, relaxed. She starts to speak when another violent trembling begins in her thighs.

JACK. Go along with it. Keep belly breathing, deep.

She lifts her bottom from the floor again. Another orgasm follows, freer and more full of movement than the first.

JACK. Make some noise as you breathe.

At first Jean grunts with each breath, then changes to a musical moan as her body and pelvic movements become deeper and spontaneous. Her third and fourth orgasm are deeply sensual, slow, with strong movements through her whole body. Even after five

<21>

orgasms the uncontrollable trembling continues. Tiny sweat droplets dot her forehead and upper lip, which is also trembling. She is getting very tired.

JACK. (*putting a hand on her shoulder*) That's good, real good. Just let your feet slide down and breathe normally. You've done great.

The group is quiet, everyone is feeling drained by Jean's experience. She lies limp, completely unselfconscious. Like five tidal waves her strong orgasms have washed away all taboos and muscle blocks. Jean stretches a nice long stretch and opens her eyes.

JACK. How do you like your dream?

JEAN. I see why I wanted to be in the driver's seat when the trooper came.

JACK. What does the trooper say now?

JEAN. Well, he's here to help you. (*smiling*)

JACK. Let's stop here ... I'm a little dizzy myself.

COMMENTARY

Jean has made contact with her frozen sexual assets and has unthawed them. She and I have used our combined awareness to guide her life energy through changes to a healthy release. That's one way to describe Gestalt therapy. Often I use key words plus body awareness to trigger the emotional reaction that is needed to complete the life pattern, or Gestalt.

Key Words   **+**   Awareness
of   Emotional   **=** Completed
body action   Reaction   Gestalt

<22>

Daddy, I hate you	+	Hitting the Pillow	Anger	= I am not a helpless child. I am a grown man, like my father.

Let's work out this illustration. I am uncomfortable around my father. I don't know why I am uptight around him. My therapist tells me to hit a pillow and yell, "Daddy, I hate you." At first this seems silly but suddenly I feel tremendous rage and tear the pillow apart. The anger was there all the time, tied up in the muscles of my arms and shoulders. The words "I hate you" plus the body movements of hitting, while the therapist takes the blame for what I'm doing, allow me to feel the emotions that have been too dangerous to feel up to now. I break through my fear, get rid of the rage left over from childhood, and take a new look at the old man. As a bonus, I get all that energy that was tied up and frozen in my muscles to use any way I want to.

Some energies, some gestalts are too deep to be triggered by words alone. Dr. Alexander Lowen developed bioenergetics theory and practice to meet this problem. Although I am not trained in this therapy, I use a few of its tools in my own therapy kit. I notice that I send more and more people to Dr. Lowen as my knowledge of the body increases. Please don't hold him responsible for what I say here, for I've never even read his books. Don't tell him that, or if you do, add I've never read all of Fritz Perls's either. I've read most of *In and Out the Garbage Pail* by Fritz, which has lots of amusing pictures and reads very easily.

In Gestalt therapy I am all for the person to have a Now experience of their unfinished personality business, for unfinished gestalts are constantly pushing to be finished. Freud called this the "repeti-

<23>

tion compulsion." I call it the "merry-go-round principle," but he named it first, so let's settle for "unfinished business." Basically, we're afraid. We're all scared children who can't get close to that horrible unfinished business. The big strong therapist takes our hands and half coaxes us, half drags us up to our fear, and alacazam! The fear turns out to be imaginary!

I learned this principle the first time I took LSD. As I was experiencing an incredible sense of beauty listening to Beethoven's Choral Symphony, a frightening bat-like monster appeared in my mind. I started to run away, panicking. Then I felt love and reassurance from God saying, "Go toward it." I did, despite my fear, and the monster vanished. In its place was an awesomely tender, beautiful triple image: a great Gothic cathedral interior, pillars reaching upward to groined arches; a majestic redwood forest standing free in the wind; and the body of a woman. Approach your fear and it will vanish. You will pass through your frozen implosive self, enter and overcome death, emerge into life and joy.

How are muscle patterns jammed? Imagine you are listening to the radio. Two or three stations are coming over the same channel so you hear the strongest one pretty well and get that message, but the other weak stations interfere so you can't get the whole message. Similarly, two messages, or three or four, will be in your muscles at once, the strongest coming through but the others interfering. Take another example: the kid who shuffles and drags his feet on the way to grammar school. He kicks trees and curbs and tin cans. His actions are saying, "I have to go to school," next, "I'll plant my feet right here and not go!" last, "I'd like to kick Mother for forcing me to go when I don't want to!" All together, pity Daddy's shoe bill! All these conflicting messages create friction and inefficiency. With start-stop, left-right, up-down, go-don't go, yes-no signals coming in all at once, no wonder a person feels chronic fatigue, malaise, headache, and all the other symptoms the TV medicine man promises to cure. We're all driving with our brakes on!

<24>

In your body, the strongest message keeps the other messages from coming through but can't keep them from pushing to be completed. Find out for yourself the next time you need to sneeze. Don't sneeze. Fight the tickle for five minutes as the sneeze impulse fights to be expressed, discharged. Then, the next time, go ahead and sneeze a nice big sneeze. AH-CHOOOOO! And it's over with, finished, done for, ready for the next gestalt, for new business.

In Jean's dreamwork, I block her usual muscle patterns by putting her into a position that sets up an unusual strain on her legs and torso, making the muscles get tired. As they tire, they lose the ability to respond to the usual signals in the usual way and begin to let go all the held-back tensions at once. Jean is a well brought up, very decent young woman who learned as she grew up that sexual feelings are to be kept tightly controlled. She does this by holding back, tightening up the muscles in her thighs, vagina, and stomach. This is truly being "uptight." Sure, a lot of people are sexually "liberated" (whatever that means) but a lot more still believe in and live by a more re-strained sexual code. Then too, many of us may have "liberated" beliefs, but the old restricting code still hangs on in our bodies. That restraint is *real*, those muscles are straining, working, getting tired, hurting, but managing to keep those sexual feelings from getting through to the head office, to awareness. So Jean can honestly say, "I'm a good woman, I'm faithful to my husband, I don't have sexy feelings. I'm not the kind of woman who wants to be turned on by every good-looking male she meets." And those muscles keep straining away until it all comes out in a dream.

The dream-Jean says, "I need more sexual release; I need to fuck. I need to make fucking movements and feel beautiful, relaxed sexual feelings. I'll dream I meet a gallant, sexy man whom I'll have to obey, so it's all right if we fuck. He makes me obey, so I don't even have to feel guilty." Through the dream-Jean's message, I guide the wake-Jean to muscle release and fuller awareness. Do I hear you say, skeptical reader, "Fine. You had fun and she had herself some fun and the crowd got to see a good show. OK, but where's the psychiatric

<25>

treatment, what difference will this experience make tomorrow, next week, next year?" Well, for Jean herself, I can't speak directly. The next two days of the workshop she was open, happy, social. I haven't worked with her since, so more than that I can't say. Most of the people I encounter after a workshop experience of this intensity tell me they've changed for the better. This much body release unlocks the door that was locked during late childhood and adolescence. It won't be locked again unless the person chooses to do so. Of course, Jean isn't going to become a *belle du jour*, a housewife-prostitute, simply because her sexual function is now more fully available to her. She will probably enjoy her husband more and get more of a charge when she sees a well-built man on the beach. She is much less likely to become one of those middle-aged ladies who ban books from libraries because the author spelled fuck, f-u-c-k, rather than f**k. Anything more is up to Jean, who is now *aware* of herself in a way she was not before.

<26>

3

The Wolf Girl Nightmare

I am privileged to hold a workshop in Oklahoma City, where I graduated from medical school twenty-six years ago. Before the workshop I drive north to Perry to see my Aunt Ella, my mother's oldest sister. Perry and Aunt Ella have changed little. Driving around the town square, I am eight years old again. Even the filling station attendants haven't changed. They are as slow to tilt their chairs forward off the rear legs and come outside their dusty offices as I remembered then. And the people haven't changed greatly in Oklahoma City, either. Oklahoma City is still the home of conscientiously friendly people who still believe in the great myths of the American past. I enjoy Oklahoma City, but I don't try to go home again.

The workshop is arranged by two friends from the medical school. They are both major culture change agents, in a pleasant, busy-bee-pollinating-from-flower-to-flower manner. Our workshop is a gracious, large private home whose elevated hearth burns warmly against the winter-stripped oaks and gray winter clouds. I feel that

<27>

warm, family-at-home atmosphere I associate with Oklahoma. The neighborliness is underlined by a small dog that roams through the room while we work, and the six-month-old baby being nursed by her mother. I have a severe bout of the Asiatic flu, which reaches its peak the day the workshop ends.

Patty, a slender brunette in bouffant hairstyle, works on this last day of the workshop. Up to this point she has had little to say. She asks to work, then settles down in the hot seat.

PATTY. I have a nightmare to work on. First let me give you some background. (*her voice has a dry, monotonous, plains twang.*) For all my life I've been afraid of wolves . . . maybe they have some symbolic meaning for me. It started when I was a child — fear and nightmares about wolves. And the extreme was this one I had last summer. So: I am in a sort of like on a plain. And sort of semi-arid, colorless, dried-up-looking bush here and there. There is, ah, a big building, sort of like a gymnasium, out in the middle of the plain. And I am going there. It seems like some other people - the only person I remember is my father — are there. On the bottom floor, kind of down in the basement, is, ah, this whole sealed-off, filled-with-wolves area. In the dream I know that the story about the building is that it was invaded by wolves, and it wasn't possible to chase them out, so they just sealed it off. I feel awfully silly (*half-laughing*). I don't recall what was on the third floor, I don't remember. And I can remember going through the building and being on the first level, and taking an elevator that was very, very scary. I wouldn't even stop on the second floor. There was this elaborate pathway the elevator took to avoid it. Such a feeling of fear and awesomeness. My God, what is in there! I was absolutely frozen with fear; I woke up just paralyzed. (*tone is half recitation, half genuine feeling*) There was some other stuff that is very hazy — something about traveling across the plain, and my father, but I feel the building is very symbolic to me.

JACK: All right. Talk to the building, please. Put it right in the chair. I'm feeling really toxic with the flu. In no condition for any

<28>

fancy maneuvers. Probably we'll have to cover a number of the dream features — the building, father, the wolves, the elevator — so let's start with the most obvious.

PATTY. I know you are me, but I don't know what you mean. I can guess, but I'm not sure. I want to know what you are about. I want to know what this big secret is.

JACK. *Your* big secret.

PATTY. *Your* big secret . . . I'm irritated that you are all locked up. (*voice falls*)

JACK. Be the building.

PATTY. (*clears throat, changes chairs*)

JACK. How do you experience yourself as the building?

PATTY. (*embarrassed laugh*) I don't.

JACK. What are you experiencing now?

PATTY. I think mostly avoidance.

JACK. OK. Let's say to Patty, "I'm avoiding you." Does that feel correct?

PATTY as building. I'm avoiding you, Patty.

JACK. How does that feel?

PATTY as building. I don't want you to learn anything about me. I like being able to scare you. If you knew about me, I couldn't have fun any more. (*right hand pulls her nose*)

JACK. What do you feel as you pull your nose? Do that again. What does it feel like?

PATTY. It feels good!

JACK. Feels good! Did anyone ever pull your nose?

PATTY. No, I don't think so.

JACK. OK, be Patty again.

<29>

PATTY. (*changes chairs*) Well, I don't like something in me I don't know anything about. I think I catch a glimpse of you every now and then. I have an idea what you are about. Part of this is preconceived. I've thought about this dream before. It's interpretation.

JACK. Uh-huh. Well, ask the building if your interpretation is correct.

PATTY. Shall I tell her what I think she is?

JACK. Uh-huh.

PATTY. Well, I think you are a lot of people, all wrapped up in one big bag. You are a witch, and . . . you're a goblin, and my mother. You're part of me . . . that wants . . . to take over my life and ruin it. You're all the ways I scare myself. I don't know what you were in the beginning, but that's what you are now.

JACK. Be the building again.

PATTY as building. (*voice higher and childish*) Ha, ha, ha, you'd really like to know . . . (*mocking*).

JACK. How do you feel as the building?

PATTY as building. I'm in control. When you're not looking, I grab you . . . (*childish, mocking*) and I do what I want to do . . . and I'm very clever . . . and it'll take you a long time to find out who I am and what to do with me . . . (*voice becomes adult again*) Yuch! (*laughing and disgusted*)

A beautiful example of a childhood partial personality split off at an early age and maintaining semiautonomy as the principal personality becomes adult. The question is, how much energy is attached or invested in this little piece of unfinished business that comes to the surface in wolf fears and nightmares? And that, in turn, depends on how much fear went into causing the personality development to get hung up at this age, plus how much satisfaction Patty gets out of playing Little Lulu.

<30>

JACK. What's your right foot doing?

PATTY. Reaching . . . hmmm.

JACK. Ask your right foot what it's reaching for.

PATTY. What are you reaching for?

PATTY as right foot. Holding her back. Keeping her from getting into that bad place again.

JACK. OK, hold her back, say, "Stay away!"

PATTY as right foot. (*adult voice*) Stay away. I don't want you to go there any more. (*voice becomes childish, laughs*) Ha (*giggle*) . . . you look like a turd under a dark bridge.

JACK. A lovely simile . . .

This kid is tougher than I thought. No wonder grown-up Patty has such a bad time with her. Looks like she's not going to lie down and die very quickly.

PATTY. (*adult voice*) There was a day I couldn't laugh. You had control of me quite frequently, but now I'm a lot wiser than you. I'm not very good prey to you, but I'm tired of wasting any time on you. I don't need you any more.

JACK. OK, stand up. Now go into the second floor. Go into the whole house.

PATTY. (*stands up, looking perplexed; adult voice*) I feel silly. I feel silly playing this.

JACK. Say to the house, "I feel silly playing your game."

This is an important technical point. Often the response is directed at the gestalt guide (the therapist). Turn that response

<31>

where it belongs, that is, to the projected concept — in this instance, the house.

PATTY. I feel silly playing your game . . . I should have better sense . . . (*long pause*) I'm, I'm afraid to . . . Well, the first floor is a nice place . . . music and a lot of people, good food and laughter . . . a lot of life is here on the first floor. But it is underground and I don't like that . . . It, it ought to be . . .

JACK: Speak to the house — *you* ought to be . . .

PATTY. *You* ought to be on ground level so the light would shine in . . . and you're kind of, well, it'd be more cheerful if there were some windows with light shining in . . . (*sadly*) OK, that's the first floor . . . (*her voice is excited and hesitant — half-scared, half-laughing*) Well, I have to go up to the second floor. (*long pause*) In my *dream* I skirted the second floor, went around it in the elevator, and climbed through some chambers. But I had the feeling I was courting danger . . . I feel like I want to sit down for the second floor . . . (*sighs*) I don't know if you're a fantasy, or if you're really there . . . I don't know if I'm really afraid of you, or just think I'm afraid of you.

JACK. Be the second floor and reply. Better lie flat. Floors usually lie flat.

PATTY as second floor. (*lying down*) You're not as afraid of me as you used to be. I did used to be real (*voice weakening*) . . . my power is declining. (*voice fading away*)

JACK. How do you feel as the second floor?

PATTY as second floor. Sort of like the witch in the Wizard of Oz when she melts . . .

JACK. The Wicked Witch of the West?

PATTY as second floor (*voice very faint*) She's been around a long time . . .

JACK. *I've* been around a long time . . .

<32>

PATTY as second floor. I've been around a long time . . . but I don't really feel like I need to be anymore.

PATTY. Right now I don't feel scared of you (*sighs. Sounds a little sad*)

My source tells me this witchy second floor is mother. Still, our purpose here is not insight for Patty or satisfied curiosity for Jack. We're out to skewer this nightmare by supporting Patty in moving through her fear and out the other side, into greater life. The sad note is that familiar nostalgia on leaving childhood: "Be It Ever So Horrid, at Least It's Home."

JACK. Are there any wolves around?

PATTY. I'm having a funny experience . . . I'm not sure I'm avoiding, but I feel a cold presence. I feel cold, and it's like I can visualize them, but I'm not sure they are here, that I'm really into it.

JACK. What do you visualize?

PATTY. Yeah, there are wolves here. But they're not doing anything. They've backed away.

JACK. Are you willing to confront the wolves?

PATTY. (*pause*) Yeah . . . You can't kill me . . . (*softly*) I won't let you kill me . . . (*little dog barks, wuff-wuff . . . group breaks into laughter. Patty laughs softly*)

JACK A little psychodrama (*chuckles*). What does the wolf say to you? Be the wolf, confront Patty.

PATTY as wolf. Oh, I've had so much fun with you . . . (voice pleasant, not mean or fierce) scaring you, making you afraid of the dark and all kinds of things . . . making you think you are crazy . . . I really can't do anything to you . . . I'm only here because you let me stay here . . . I don't have any teeth, I can't bite you. You've needed me . . . (*sigh*) . . . yeah. (*tone of decision*) Mother, mother . . .

<33>

JACK. The wolf is mother?

PATTY. No, as long as I let the wolf and all that it represents, you know, hang around . . . and control me and scare me, then I can, I can be what I think my mother wanted me to be. Something she wanted to put off on me. Some trip she laid on me, you know. But I just don't, just don't *need* all that trip any more. (*decisively*)

That sums up one kind of parentally induced neurotic trip in one paragraph. Patty sees that at one level she uses the neurosis to remain scared and dependent, in order to be a "good girl," so mother will love her. Our contemporary phrase is "She laid a trip on me."

JACK. I tell you what I want you to do. I want you to chase all the wolves out of that second story (*Patty gasps, as if startled*) then open all the windows. Go up to the third story and do the same thing . . . OK?

PATTY (*giggles very softly*) OK.

JACK. In other words, clean house.

Patty laughs, claps her hands together, delighted, childlike. Her humor is contagious as, without a word, she begins vigorously shooing the wolves out, then rushes around the imaginary room, violently throwing open the imaginary windows. The group laughs delightedly.

JACK. You're feeling your nose again. Is your nose cold?

PATTY. (*voice high with humor*) I don't know. I'm hanging onto my nose.

JACK. Ask your nose what's happening.

PATTY. What's happening, nose?

PATTY as nose. I want to feel a connection with you, hand.

<34>

JACK. Let nose and hand have a conversation.

PATTY as hand. I'm somewhat unsure, and a little bit frightened, and, and I, I want to, ah, have your support, and to know you are here with me, that we are all together . . . and I want to give you the support . . . I want to let you know I am here.

JACK. How does your nose feel now?

PATTY as nose. Thank you. I haven't chased out all the wolves yet . . . got to get them out of here . . . (*laughs with delight*) ohh. (*voice commanding*) Wolves! You've had this floor long enough! I'm tired of cleaning up your dirty messes and all that noise . . . and I'm just tired of the space you take up. I want to use this space! I've got things I want to put on this floor. You're going to have to get out. So, please just pick yourselves up, and GET OUT . . . (*aside, in a strong voice*) They're leaving . . .

JACK. Open all the windows.

PATTY. (*throwing windows open, then in musing tone of housewife doing spring cleaning*) I think I'll have a bay window here. I've always wanted a bay window. Open up a bay window here . . . that really lets the air in, that's clean there . . . a lot nicer now.

JACK. Can you go to the third floor and finish the job?

PATTY. I think the third floor is a . . . the whole floor is like that out there, a terrace . . . all open . . . I don't see anything else up there, it's just nice.

JACK. The whole house is clear?

PATTY. Well, I've got to bring the bottom floor up . . . put it on ground level.

MASCULINE VOICE from group. You want to bring the whole basement up to ground level?

PATTY . Yeah.

VOICE. Boy, that's a job! (*laughter*)

<35>

PATTY. I jack it up, I don't want to dig around it ... jack it up ... I don't have to call anybody. I can just do it. Put the jack here. (*suits action to words, starts jacking away as on an auto*) Got to turn on the electricity, go all around ... there!

JACK. Pretty nice house, eh?

PATTY. Yeah. (*speaks to house*) You're got lots of sunshine coming in. I like you.

PATTY as house. I feel sad. (*begins weeping — somewhat phony feminine voice*) I've lost a part of myself, and I feel a little bit sad ...

JACK. Patty, come back and be you.

PATTY. (*her own voice*) I feel excitement now.

JACK. Where do you feel the excitement?

PATTY. All of me. *I* have a lot of possibilities, a lot of me to be now. I'm not sad. I'm excited and happy.

JACK. Beautiful! Let's stop here, OK?

PATTY. OK ... thank you, Jack.

COMMENTARY

The most important dreams we have are what we call "recurring" dreams; those that we seem to have over and over again with minor modifications. These dreams seem to be insistently pleading to be "let out," to be understood, to be integrated. More often than not, recurring dreams are nightmares. Loosely speaking, any dream accompanied by fear, especially on awakening, is a nightmare. But the specific quality of nightmares, even more than fear, is enormous frustration.

<36>

Patty has been frustrated a long time. The building in her dream represents her life, and she has been frustrated by her childhood teachings from fully living and exploring herself.

Patty's life is content as long as she lives underground. When she attempts to emerge, to separate from the security of her mother, her fears restrain her from fully occupying her adult life space (the second floor of her dream). I don't have any ready explanation for the third floor or terrace. It is available to her. Perhaps I would do better to insist that she go up and check the third floor out.

Patty has already done some hard work on herself before this dream. We added some energy in the form of some needed direction and support. Is the job completed? Is this particular business of Patty's finished? Optimistically, I think yes. Patty's entire energy level is much higher when she has finished the dream. Her voice has changed from a drab controlled monotone to a lively verbal sparkle. Patty now has a lot more space to live in, to be Patty in. Less of her is tied up in no longer useful childish controls.

<37>

4

The Soundless Flute and the Empty Coffin

This dream comes from Esalen at Big Sur, in late summer of 1971. I am recovering from hepatitis, tire easily, and lack energy to carry people beyond themselves. The ocean, a sunny purple, lies across the highway from us. The air is filled with the aroma from green dry slopes — warm sage and wild rosemary. Our meeting room opens onto the swimming pool where the clear blue water contrasts with the brown or pink or white body of an occasional bather. Before sundown clothing is superfluous except to go to the dining room or out into the parking lot. The setting greatly reduces those tense currents common to city life that must be cleared away before the deep essential forces can be felt.

Amos is a New Yorker, middle-aged like myself, successful and caught in a profession that no longer gives him rewards other than a comfortable living. He sits quietly for several days, a courteous, rather noteworthy figure. I am stirred to invite him to work one quiet morning while the late-comers step over feet and make their way into

<39>

cushiony corners. He responds to my raised eyebrows by settling in the hot seat, next to mine.

JACK. OK, Amos?

AMOS. (*in the form of a mild challenge*) Why am I here?

JACK. Why are you here? All right . . . No, ask Dave over there that.

AMOS. (*his tone changed*) Dave, why am I here?

DAVE. Why are you here? You have a problem to work on, I imagine.

AMOS. I have a problem to work on — what kind of problem, Dave?

DAVE. Perhaps a dream, or something really bothering you.

AMOS. (*reflecting on the answer*) I don't have much real . . . I don't feel myself much, somehow. As if I didn't really have much important to present of myself somehow. A problem to work on. A . . . a . . . distinct problem to work on . . . I didn't feel that.

JACK. Change to present tense, "I don't . . . "

AMOS. I don't feel I have a distinct problem to work on. So I simply watch and listen. And see other people work. And see you work. And with it I'm very absorbed sometimes. And some of it comes right back to me. It resonates to me. And ah . . . but, it's not complete.

JACK. Stop. Change the "it" to "I."

My low energy shows. I haven't the resources to be polite *and* directive. Hepatitis makes me very "liver-ish," an old idiom from the centuries when English gentlemen drank so much they had cirrhosis by forty.

AMOS. . . . but *I'm* not complete.

<40>

JACK. Say that again.

AMOS. But, I'm not complete.

JACK. How does that feel?

AMOS. Ah, hmm ... I have an old dream, an old dream.

JACK. (*disdaining further chit-hat*) Right now, tell your dream in the present tense, "I am ... "

AMOS. I am your dream ... Tell the dream?

This boy is *good*, see how he puts out the bait, then switches?

JACK. Go ahead. That's an interesting beginning. (*I'm off balance, so bullshit*)

AMOS. I'll just switch it around I guess. (*mumbles audibly*) Why hadn't you asked to be presented? (*apparently talking to the dream*) Why hadn't you been more persistent? Why don't you make me recognize you? Why don't you make me declare you to the others?

A corollary to the Golden Rule: As you do unto others, so will you do unto yourself. Amos has to be top dog with his own dream. This is typical top dog speaking.

JACK. All right, sit over here and be the dream now.

AMOS as dream. You never ask for anything. You don't ask for yourself and you don't ask for me. You're content to let things slide by. To let time go by. Nothing really counts. You can always do it again. You can always dream another dream. And forget that one too ...

Hear the bitterness of the rejected? The dreams that never get beyond fantasy? The possibilities stillborn?

<41>

JACK. What are you feeling?

AMOS. I feel my face a little bit. A little bit of tightness. Like grimacing to tears. Something like that. A little bit of something. You're an old dream, but I think you have meaning for me. And I can dream other dreams that will give me the same message. But, you're a single dream. I'm even proud of you. And I recognize what you have to say, even before I go into working on you. But if I . . . deal with you directly, if I touch you, you'll tell me more. Even though I see what you show me, I'll see it better. I am your dream, which is an old dream.

JACK. (*motioning to chair opposite*) "I am an old dream . . . "

Amos seems to be extremely introspective; I accentuate the structure of the gestalt dialogue, the chair, differentiating between Amos and his projected dream and so forth, so he won't get lost or lose me in his meanderings.

AMOS. I am an old dream. Tell them about me. I'm at what seems to be a large outdoor ceremony. There are many people, it's like a Japanese ceremony. Everyone is wearing a black robe or kimono. They are facing a shelter of some sort. A shrine. I'm kneeling. There's someone kneeling near me. I have in front of me at my knees a little log. Like a piece of firewood or something. A log. And I settle myself. There's someone there that's doing the same thing . . . to the side. The log . . . and I don't know if this is retrospect . . . the log seems to be petrified. It's like a real old hunk of wood. It's like a facsimile even. Something created or simply hardened. I feel a song coming out of it. I feel it very strongly, in my chest. Notes. And I recognize it. It's as if I'm trying to blow a flute but it's not a flute. It's right out here. It's coming right out . . . it's very strong. I know the notes to it. And then I'm some place else, off to the side away from the ceremony. There are a lot of shells. A lot of shells and in these shells there are a lot of instruments. Flutes. Very nice lovely flutes.

<42>

And maybe French horns. I reach for them and see them and touch them. And I have a choice. A choice, a whole range of choices. I just take one or the other. I notice that there are some that are kind of tinny. Like tin whistles. Or something like that. And I pick up a kazoo. A black kazoo. It seems to be made of crepe paper or something, just a flimsy little thing. And I look off to the side and I see a little procession. There are several figures . . . black robes again. Walking slowly. And they are carrying overhead a coffin . . . And that coffin, I see after a bit, is really made of crepe paper. It's just like crepe paper. It's very flimsy. It's not even a real coffin. Part of the ceremony. It's nice and soothing. A lovely pageant. It's not a . . . it's crepe paper. Nothing inside. (*pause*) Somehow the telling of it is also not real. It's a nice little presentation. A nice little thing. It's not a . . . not a . . . you know . . . it's nice theater. But that's about it.

JACK. (*after a reflective pause*) Say to your dream what you just said.

AMOS. Well, it's very interesting . . .

JACK. "You're very interesting . . . "

AMOS. You're very interesting. Nice piece of work. Quite interesting. Nice shape to it. Have an interesting theme . . . and uh . . . uh . . . so what. So it's interesting. So you're very nice and I get your point. Fine. I know what you're telling me. There's only one point that hit me in the gut. And that wasn't saying much. It was just something that I felt. The rest of it has been just an interesting picture. Thank you. (*sarcastically*)

JACK. Be the dream.

Apparently some tension is building up. Amos's controlled, suave surface is showing some stress marks.

AMOS as dream. (*louder, with irritation*) I didn't ask to come. You asked me. You had me. (*pause, clenching his jaw*)

<43>

JACK. Can you feel your resentment as the dream?

AMOS as dream. I'm fucking angry!

AMOS. (*suddenly deflated*) You told me to tell it to Art, well I did! I said to him, "I'm angry." I told Art I'm angry. (*his anger is spent, he is anxious*)

JACK. What's happening now? Where's your anger?

AMOS. It's in my head. It's that shape there becoming something else now. It's not anger, it's just warmth and a little tension. (*to the dream*) I know I made you. And I think it's a good job. But I don't think it went far enough. I didn't work on you hard enough. I had plenty of time to do it. And if I like you so much as a dream, as a statement, why didn't I work on you? Why didn't I use you?

JACK. Hear how reasonable your voice is now? As Amos you're calm and reasonable. As Amos's dream you're resentful and angry. Be the dream again. Take another breath.

Amos has been breathing in a shallow way. He isn't in touch with his source of life, his breathing.

AMOS as dream. If I had so much to say to you a year and a half ago, *why the fuck didn't you listen*! (*pause, breathing heavily*) Why do you sit there so accepting, so calm? So outwardly calm. Why do you let time go by?

Why, why, why — the mind inquiry, give me data, give me the material to come up with the answer. And there is no "answer." There is only the process, the continually changing configuration of life. Amos is stuck in his mind, alienated from his sensory experiences. The only way we contact our world and ourselves is through our senses. The person who turns off his senses cuts himself off from experience as surely as a blind man or a deaf man.

<44>

JACK. (*at the same time that I give this instruction to Amos I have the realization that I am failing him, that I should steer him away from his customary use of words and into some body action. I am, however, too weary to react immediately to my intuition*) Make a statement, not a question.

AMOS as dream. (*without emphasis*) Don't let time go by. Don't be accepting.

JACK. Hear what happened? When you have to take a position you lose your aliveness.

AMOS as dream. Work me . . . Use me . . . So you can use yourself.

AMOS. It sounds like moralism. It sounds moralistic.

JACK. (*hoping that some energy will emerge in the moralizing side of Amos*) So be moralistic. Tell Amos how to be. Yeah, go on. Be moralistic. Tell Amos "You've lost your anger so you take refuge in being a moralist." Moralists are people who have lost the ability to sin anyway. Most people who pass sex laws can't fuck. So be moralistic, tell Amos how he *should* be — "You should be such and such."

AMOS as moralist. I find it hard to say any shoulds. (*a common example of compliance in Gestalt-oriented people is a reluctance to say "should," as they know that they shouldn't say "should"*) I-you should be a good boy. And do your work. And do as people tell you to do. And do as the analyst tells you to do. And do as Jack Downing tells you. And do your job. Sit in that chair. Get to work on your dreams and do a good job. That's it.

 VOICE from group. Bravo! (*scattered applause from the group*)

JACK. Do I detect resentment in that itemized list?

AMOS. A certain amount, a measured amount. A carefully calculated amount that won't get me into trouble.

JACK. Like with who?

AMOS. Like with you.

<45>

JACK. Like with you, that's who, huh? I find you a pleasant companion in chitchat. May I offer you a mild escape from this dream you find so tedious?

AMOS. I don't see why not.

JACK. Always cautious Amos. All right. I offer you the unique opportunity of becoming any person you wish to be, and of experiencing whatever you wish as him. Take your time.

AMOS. (*sits with eyes looking downward, from time to time biting the corner of his mouth*) I know, the Beat novelist, I'll be him.

JACK. Who's this?

AMOS. Jack Kerouac, the guy who . . .

JACK. He's dead now?

AMOS. Yea. But there's a film I just saw called *Pull My Daisy* that has the same sound, exact sound of my dream. The same singsong tone and the whole bit. It's all these empty words. Being said and being dismissed as they're said. Doesn't really mean anything. He says, "Holy, Holy. Can a ring be Holy? Can Mama be Holy? Can I be Holy? Holy. Holy. It's a bitch. It's nothing. Great." Just sounds. And it's great gibberish and tumult. And nothing counts and nothing means anything. But it's fun. (*Amos is lively, even a slight smile on his face. He's turned on, in a minimal way*)

JACK. Ah. You're kind of happy now, no?

AMOS. (*going right back down into the pit*) Ah, the same old bullshit.

JACK. You've had enough of being Jack Kerouac?

AMOS. That was all I wanted. Just the shell of the experience.

JACK. Oh, can you feel the shell descending over you?

<46>

I feel I'm getting exactly nowhere. Amos doesn't want any part of my messing around with his psyche. So, I'm getting curious. What is he doing?

AMOS. Not, no . . . it's kind of funny . . . maybe . . . I was sort of contemplating that the general black-grays of the dream . . .

JACK. Speak to the dream, "your black-grays . . . "

AMOS. Your black-grays and false pomp and lovely ceremonial gestures are kind of empty. There's nothing much to you. Lovely as you may be . . . as a painting or as a film kind of thing . . . artfully directed . . . you're just ceremony . . . empty gesture. You don't really get in on deep things. You appear to be deep but you're not deep. You appear to be valuable and important, and a key and have stuff. You're touching on life and death and yet you're not life and death. And you really aren't touching on life and death, you're only touching about something that's touching. You're describing something, but you're not that something. You're not even a description of something. You're a description of a description of something.

JACK. What would you like to do with your dream?

At this point, I'm convinced that I can do nothing other than go along with Amos. His lack of substance, of the stuff of reality, is beyond my ability to generate a pattern, a gestalt.

AMOS. A flicker of something came to my head. But I couldn't hold onto it. It's as if it's not my dream's fault really, that I can't find myself.

JACK. Select from the dream the part that interests you most.

AMOS. I much more . . . really loved the flute. Though I can't play it, I want to.

JACK. All right, speak to the flute. Say just that.

<47>

AMOS. I love you, wood. And the people who made you. The person who made you. Because he loved you when he made you, and it was part of him. You're well made, and now you're silent. I love to touch you. (*long pause while his hands softly stroke the imagined instrument*) I'm afraid I won't learn how to play you. (*pause*) I have something to say in you. But I don't know how to use you, I don't know how I can learn. I don't think I could learn by myself, so you'll just remain a nice object with warm wood tones, lying on the shelf. A half-dozen shapes, sizes, possibilities, my friends may learn to play.

JACK. What is your left hand doing to your right hand?

AMOS. It's aimless.

JACK. Let your left hand speak, "I'm aimless."

AMOS as left hand. I just realized that I'm aimless as can be. I'm disjointed and aimless. I have no direction. I can't make a coherent pattern. I just push myself once in a while to tell you that I'm here. That's all that I can do. Give you a nudge just to remind you that I'm around. Clumsy blob, I have possibilities even though they're spread apart and disjointed and . . . (*he speaks thickly, tears are visible in his eyes*)

AMOS. (*speaking to his left hand, bitterly*) You are just a club, less than I am. (*long pause, tears but no sound from Amos*)

JACK. (*placing my hand on Amos's shoulder*) What does your right hand say?

AMOS as right hand. I've been a wall to you. I want to look ordinary like everyone else. I'm sorry this is hard work . . . to make you be . . . to make you function. I'm out of practice. I can't do that.

AMOS. There's unfulfillment in this too. There's a giving in. A disappointment. Like an I-told-you-so. My life is speaking to me, to my disappointments. (*long pause; Amos turns his face away from me*)

<48>

JACK. One more image. I want you to be the coffin. Lie down and be the paper coffin. (*Amos lies on the floor, a feeling of solemnity as he closes his eyes*)

AMOS as coffin. I'm being carried slowly. And the wind's whipping around the edges of me and unfurling the covering, the paper. The frame, my frame is being exposed. Cleanly made, but it won't support anything, there's nothing in between. Only a frame, nicely shaped, well put together as a frame, but without function. When the paper's torn away you can see I'm not a coffin.

I look somber enough and dignified enough to pass for what I'm supposed to be. What I represent to others I do well enough as long as I'm protected from the buffeting of wind and stuff like that. My job is limited. I just do that ceremony and can be thrown away or used in another ceremony. I enjoy looking at me, at the design of me. But I can't do anything by myself, so someone will have to do it for me. Someone has to bear me as a coffin, cover me or uncover me. I'm not a very good coffin. I don't even look like a coffin now. I'm becoming something else, kind of an elaborated wooden sculpture. (*pause*) That's a little better, at least I'm becoming something other people can enjoy by looking at me. (*long pause; his breathing becomes deeper and slower*)

JACK. What are you experiencing now?

AMOS. Sort of calm. A little bit of sadness. A little bit of emptiness.

JACK. I feel like stopping here. Is that all right with you?

AMOS. Sure. (*long pause*) I keep bringing things down. Down, down, down. Kind of a role I play. To bring things down. Quiet, serious, empty. Very empty. Very empty.

JACK. A nice artistic end . . . and empty. (*I clasp his hand, he responds with brief, formal pressure*)

<49>

COMMENTS ON AMOS' DREAMWORK

I sense in Amos that lack of life, that overly civilized smoothness that denotes the man who for many years has despaired of finding true freedom and so settles for lack of conflict. An astute word manipulator, Amos is able to distract himself and others from his underlying lack of life. Beneath his sophisticated exterior, Amos is depressed, quietly empty. It is a dangerous condition, a condition that often results in failing to awaken some Sunday morning with two empty bottles of sedatives next to the bed. (And his everyday friends saying, "What in the world made him do that? He had everything going for him.")

Upon reviewing my dream work with Amos I am far from satisfied with how I have handled him and the progress he has made. My basic error was in allowing him to continue his word manipulation game. I should have steered, pushed, forced hIm into his own body, into an awareness of his breathing, and so on. I should have worked harder to help him avoid the sterility of his usual game playing. Working with depressed people, such as Amos, is a particular drain and unfortunately I was too depressed from my own recent illness to do other than resonate to his somber vibrations. The physician was engaged in healing himself and hadn't much energy to spare. As I go along in healing, I become more and more aware that I earn my fee by having health in myself to pass on to others. When I fail to keep in balance, in contact with my own energy, I fail to give that which I have contracted to give to the other person. I have observed that many of my psychotherapist colleagues appear drained; they are excellently garbed emptinesses (much like Amos) who have nothing to give except empty directions and textbook comments. Others, deeply rooted in their families, their communities, their religions, and themselves, have love and energy to pass on, and do.

For Amos, I am particularly glad that the group is warm and the weather beautiful. The love and concern he needs are available in the camaraderie around the pool, in the back rubs and sweat-soaked

<50>

sauna sessions. The magic of Esalen wraps around him and nourishes his emptiness. He retains the essential desire to have personal contact, even if he can't feel himself as more than a fake coffin, "at least I'm becoming something other people can enjoy . . . " He feels inaccessible. But I see him quietly content, floating in the warm pool. He accepts my urging that he be massaged by the centered, meditative young women of the massage crew. I wish that there were an Esalen East for this fellow pilgrim whose way is so without substance. There isn't.

We, Amos and I, have a wry, quiet, mutual understanding. He appreciates that I haven't bullshitted him. He's empty; I acknowledge his elegantly elaborated front, his persona, and his emptiness. That is something, even though empty. Could he be helped? Yes. By working through his body, we could help Amos to reunite his instinctual biological energies with his mind, to get his guts and his head and his heart together. Talking alone is not enough. Physical experience and physical nourishment nurtured by real love and concern are required.

<51>

5

The Descent of the Holy Spirit

Only by being fully alive myself am I privileged to share the adventures of people I encounter and dreams I listen to. If my own senses are obscured, my own body, mind, and soul uncleansed, I cannot fully join the experience of another human being. I must be whole enough in my own mind, in my own self, to be able to choose love rather than hate or resentment, and in that way open myself to the beauty and experience of others.

The most soul-touching of any dream experience I have shared is with Beatrice at Bucks County. This is a prophetic dream, the first and only clear prophecy that I have been granted to share. God's love and mercy are clearly laid out.

Beatrice is a sensuous, supple lady of indeterminate age, one of those slender, ivory-skinned brunettes who step off the path of time about age thirty and refuse to cooperate with Father Time. She has the subtle air of looking directly at a man in such a way that the man

<53>

immediately knows she knows more about him than he sometimes cares to reveal.

She slips into the hot seat and I surmise from her features that she is from southeastern Europe — Hungary, Rumania, Bulgaria, somewhere in there — which she later confirms. Her eyes glisten with a hint of tears. Her legs and hands are pressed tightly together. She seems to be huddling as though seeking protection against some unseen hand. The group, not yet aware of Beatrice's intensity, is restless, buzzing, so that I am forced to call out sharply, "OK! That's it! Pipe down!"

Beatrice begins immediately. There is no need to bring her into the Now. She could not escape this moment if she wished to. You will notice that, as she narrates her dream, Beatrice uses the past tense and I do not, as I usually do, insist upon her changing to the present. In Gestalt therapy, as in everything else, the law was made for people, not people for the law.

BEATRICE. I was very turned on, in terms of feeling very close to the things around me. It was a bright sunny day. And I was lying out in this big field, and I closed my eyes. And was kind of resting. There were people around, I suppose.

All of a sudden, with my eyes closed, a shade went up. And I saw an eye. There was no longer anything outside.

I wasn't frightened and I looked at the eye. And the eye became a face. It was the most compassionate face I have ever seen. Looking at the face I became full of tenderness. And the word ... and the word "Father" came to mind. And then a part of me began to analyze. You know, the word "Father," you must be reaching for your father and what have you. But, I couldn't keep the thought. Feeling came back. And I went on a journey. (*pause*)

And then one more thought came into my mind. And the thought was that it looked like the face of Jesus. And that seems strange to me because I was born in a Jewish family, and I was raised without

<54>

any religious training. It struck me as odd, and that was the last thought, in a sense, that I had as a thought.

For then I was filled with a presence of love. Of a unity of love. I understood that there must be a loving presence. I understood about concentration camps. And how people could die. And this is what people did, but above it — I don't like to verbalize — there was this loving unity of which I was a part, that went on and on in infinity, and in circles. I understood more than I understood without thought. There was a fullness in me and I was someplace else.

Then I opened my eyes and looked up. And space was not empty. Space was filled and I was no longer afraid of spacelessness. I had been so afraid of spacelessness all my life. Words and intellect would not come into my mind. I was filled with feelings; the joy of being part of this unity. Then part of me ... I lay there for a while ... then part of me tried to get thoughts in my mind again, and analyze it. And I couldn't. I could not destroy what I was experiencing with analyzing. I tried but I couldn't. There was a glow about me.

My husband, who was there, came over and said, "You look very strange." I said, "I can't explain it, but I'm filled." Then a couple of hours later, we stopped on our journey home. I was sitting by a pool by myself. There was nobody else there. I closed my eyes and the light came on again. It went into a circle and I saw a scene that was very strange.

At first it looked like a drawing that one makes if you take salt and paste and put them on paper. You'd get a relief kind of thing. It was a shepherd, and lambs, and ... and was very peaceful. I was in another place and yet it was someplace familiar. The belief in what I felt, and the feeling of being part of the whole and for the first time in my life believing in something beyond myself because I had never been able to believe in God or anything beyond anything in life. This feeling stayed with me and I could not deny it.

The second part of the experience in my dream ... I went to a Gestalt workshop and we played a game called "Let's Build a World." We were given paper, magazines, and all kinds of things, and a table,

<55>

and clay. It was only a game, and I really couldn't get into it very much. Except that I picked up a piece of clay, put it down and said, "That's my space. I'm willing to build, but I must have my own space someplace."

The game got very involved. There was a nun there ... not in a habit ... that was very peculiar because nobody knew who anybody was, but when I embraced her for the first time I looked at her and said, "You're a nun." She said, "How do you know?" There was a ponytail down her back. I said, "I don't know."

And anyway people decided they didn't want to have war, and it was going to be a beautiful life. We were all going to live peacefully together. But as we cut out things, to include in our world, one of the things we accepted was death. We took the piece of paper ... with the word death ... we cut them and put them down on the table.

We're building this peaceful world and the first thing I know I turn around and this man has a wall built on his side. I said to him, "What do you have this wall built for?" And he says, "You can't live like that. I'm going to live behind a wall." I said, "Ah, come on. You know." He said, "If you touch that wall, you and I are going to have it out." In any event I decided I'd keep on building. The first thing I know, things are hitting the paper on the world we built. The nun said, "They're bombs, and I'm dead." I had just put down something of mine and this man had grabbed it up. I looked and I couldn't find myself. I figured, "Gee ... maybe I'm dead too." Then I thought, "I get some brownie points for being dead and what have you?" Then I got scared. Because now I knew that if I said I was dead I was going to experience something. And I knew I had to say I was dead. And I said, "I'm dead too."

I went over and joined the nun who had been bombed, killed. I felt very separate. Then she sat down. She said, "Come closer." I sat with her. And suddenly I was in another place. The noises in the room seemed to diminish, and there were lots of other people in the room. I had a feeling that wherever death is, you are not alone. I then recalled the same feeling I had in the field. I was surrounded again by

<56>

this loving feeling. I've held on to this experience and this belief and I could not deny it. Though every now and then I try to analyze it. But it just doesn't work out, trying to analyze it.

I kept those loving feelings within me for a long time. Then my daughter was killed in an automobile accident. I mean, *really* killed. Not in a dream or anything like that. It was very strange. I was in shock immediately. But you know, it's the strangest thing, because when my children have been away at times I have worried where they were. But when I was told she was dead, I knew where she was. The pain of losing her and not having her to share a life with is my loss. But I knew at that time where she was. Somehow she seemed part of this loving whole. I wondered whether it was the prophecy that at first I experienced the loving whole, and then I lost my daughter. I'm frightened now to a degree, because I need to hold on. I can't deny it, but there's a sense of feeling that I keep for a long time. I guess it's almost as if I'm still anxious to hold on to the feeling — that I'm afraid it's going to slip. I'm not sure what I'm asking for in help. Whether it's an affirmation — that such things are possible? And why this all came before my daughter's death ... and not after as a rationalization. Whether such inner journeys are possible for me in my context and my lifetime? I had no context, except that I had always been very tuned in. I want the feeling to stay ... (*pause*)

What could I say? I am overwhelmed by Beatrice's dream, by her vision, followed by her daughter's real death. Her vision had been of the eye of God, the face of God, and finally the unity of God within all of us. She had had a vision of God as our father, the loving shepherd; and then, through a vision of her own death, she had come into the company of the blessed to share with them the love of God. All this in preparation to enable her to understand and accept her daughter's eventual passing. What could *I* say? I decided to play it straight Gestalt. I sense no other course.

<57>

JACK. All right . . . Would you be willing to talk to the man you saw when you were lying in the field? To the Christ. That *was* the Christ?

BEATRICE. I suppose. (*doubtfully*)

JACK. all right, talk to the Christ. (*I point to the other chair*)

BEATRICE. (*long pause*) Someplace you have been mortal, such as I. I do not see you as idealized, perfect. I see you as a man, a human being. It's very important to me that you were a man. And lived, and grew up . . . (*pause*)

JACK. Is he there in the chair now?

BEATRICE. Not in a body.

JACK. Well, the Presence. Is the Presence there?

BEATRICE. There is a . . . I'm not sure.

JACK. Right. The Christ is in your heart. Take him out of your heart and put him in the chair.

BEATRICE. (*Long pause; Beatrice puts her hands to her breast, holding them together, then solemnly moves to the chair opposite and opens her hands*) Funny, there are two people in that chair. There is my child. And she is not alone.

JACK. Then talk to her. What's her name?

BEATRICE. Ellen.

JACK. Ellen.

BEATRICE. Ellen. You are safe. This is what you really always wanted. You were a beautiful bitch at times.

JACK. Present tense. "You are . . . "

BEATRICE. You are a bitch probably even now. In your knowledge that you loved yourself, or sought to love yourself. And wanted to feel and act. Beautiful body . . . That grew into a woman while you were still a child. And you wanted . . . want to soar. And I cannot

<58>

believe that because you are so vital ... so full of life, that you are not perhaps more you than when you were chained. (*Pause*)

JACK. Be Ellen.

BEATRICE as Ellen. Mom, we always fought. But you really saw me and I was scared that you saw me. Because I didn't understand what it was I was feeling. I resented being big, when I wanted to be little. I resented being a woman when I wanted to be a little girl. (*Pause*) I'm really zooming around. Clouds are better than motorcycles. (*Long pause*) And I can be a stone, and I can lie in the water again. And I'm smiling. I can feel you, but I can't touch you. Even though I know you want to be touched. Very strange, I feel very strange laughing with joy and crying at the same time. And I am free. I told you that I would rather live and die than never live and I lived and I died.

BEATRICE. (*long pause*) Ellen, I wasn't sure for a while, whether I wanted to die with you, whether ... But I love myself and must choose life. (*pause*) And strangely enough, when I was able to give up the dying, and come back to my own living, I could find joy again. I would like to touch you. And that's why I wouldn't bury you. That's why I held on to the box of ashes. But then I discovered that I had lost you, because you weren't in the box. And I had to give up the box and go back to my own life. In the affirmation of my own life I find you again. You're a hard-ass. I miss you. But you are ... and I and ...

JACK. What is your right foot doing? (*Foot is extending, resting on rung of opposite chair*)

BEATRICE. Touching. She's in that chair.

JACK. Do you want to ask her about the other presence in that chair?

BEATRICE. She's not alone. You're not alone Ellen. There isn't a man in that chair ... in a body. And you're not in a body. But the essence of you and the essence of that man. And all the essences are

<59>

love. I still find it hard, Ellen, not to cry so much. I think I shall remain here, in the sunlight, for a while.

JACK. What do you feel in your heart . . . in your chest?

BEATRICE. A fullness . . . part of it's pain of not being able to reach across.

JACK. Stay with the pain. Stay with that feeling without putting a label on it. Just close your eyes and experience that feeling. Experience it . . . keep breathing . . . (*pause*) Don't stop breathing, keep breathing. And keep feeling . . . don't put a label on it. (*long pause*) Breathe.

BEATRICE. The pain is going.

JACK. Keep breathing.

BEATRICE. I have an impulse . . . it's very strange, but just to go like this. (*Extends her arms upward*)

I recognize in her gesture the mudra of reception, that is, the reaching upward to God.

JACK. Do it. Do it. Receive. Up higher. That's it. A little bit higher. Now look . . . turn you head back and look up. That's it. That's it.

There is a long pause, a long long pause. I sense an indescribable feeling of ecstasy, of love and peace, surrounding Beatrice and me, surrounding all of us in the room . . . Finally . . . Thank you.

BEATRICE. (*long pause before she speaks*) What happened?

JACK. We have a word for it. Samadhi — that you are with God. (*The group is completely hushed. I turn to them*) You have just seen or felt the descent of the Holy Spirit, the Holy Ghost, which I myself had never seen before in group work such as this.

<60>

At this point my own tears clear enough for me to see that three people in the group, two women and a man, are crying openly. Beatrice is being held by a friend kneeling beside her chair. I go over to Carol who seems in need of something, of someone. I put my arm around her shoulder and hold her head gently against me. She tenses, then relaxes and allows herself to cry freely, sobbing for nearly five minutes. Then she moves away from me, to her purse, for a handkerchief. The group leaves silently, all of them except for Beatrice and me. We sit there together without speaking a single word until the luncheon bell rings. Beatrice does not go to lunch. She walks off to sit alone in the sunshine. I go to eat.

COMMENTS ON BEATRICE'S EXPERIENCE

Beatrice's dream and subsequent feelings of a loving presence were unique. A year of divine preparation for her daughter's death and for her own heightened consciousness. My professional pretensions of explanation and controlling are of little use in the face of what I can only call such "sacred moments." Fortunately, I had just completed a year of Arica training in Chile and this had prepared me by cleaning my own body and soul, so that I was able to recognize the experience for what it was — an experience transcending professional "knowledge"; an experience touching upon the supreme power, the supreme will that exists in all of us.

The technical problem with such an experience is to supply the supporting validating affirmation of the reality of such revelations. Beatrice lives in our materialistic culture which denies rather than affirms the reality of a spiritual life. As she says, "Are such things possible for me in my context and my lifetime?" What an age of disbelief that question implies. It is difficult for us to break through a lifetime of training. Trained that Up is Down and Down is Up, we all walk on our hands and salute each other with our feet. A graduate social psychotherapist, Beatrice had been taught the supremacy of the mind — so, " . . . every now and then I try to analyze it . . . it

<61>

just doesn't work out. I just don't know what it meant." We have difficulty recognizing that it means what it *is*; it *is* what Beatrice experiences. Or if you prefer that I use psychological terms, that I be more "scientific": an analyzed gestalt is devoid of the unique meaningfulness inherent in the particular configuration denoted by the particular time-space-personality sequence. Bacon, ham, and sausage do not make a pig. Two pigs make a third pig and no amount of analysis has ever changed that.

Another age might have called Beatrice "blessed," privileged to see the unseen, to experience the unknowable, to touch a part of another greater life beyond the intellectual confinements most of us have placed ourselves in. Guardians of our present intellectual age might call Beatrice "neurotic," "hysterical," "hallucinatory," "unwilling to face reality." My own experiences validate the greater reality of Beatrice's vision. There are experiences that produce happiness, wisdom, and beauty far more abundant than the concepts by which our limited personal and social lives are bound.

During the following months, Beatrice did have some difficulty reconciling her vision with the social reality of her routine life. I was unable to help her as much as I would have liked for I had returned to California. The "here today, gone tomorrow" aspect of my workshops is admittedly one drawback of them. Beatrice wrote to me and I responded, but with how much help I do not know. I urged her to participate in the Arica training that was being given in New York City, to provide herself with a foundation for the soaring spiritual peaks she had proved herself capable of experiencing. She decided not to, I suspect partially because she had absorbed all the changes she could handle at that time.

May our paths cross again. She is an exceptional human being.

<62>

6

Roger and the Dwarf Woman

As my years drift up like karmic leaf piles, I see lives fall into patterns. Some of these patterns repeat endlessly over and over again with a few modifications. The good people who come to my workshops are pretty much of a pattern: middle class, well-educated, with lively minds and good income. They seem successful and secure in their own worlds, and then they begin wondering, suspecting something is missing. Some unsatisfied animal in them is awakened and they turn their heads, thrust out their hearing; their goal: a faint suspicion of sound, the Logos, the vibration of God. "Was there something out there? Did I really hear reality? Let us see if we can see, hear if we can hear." They come to Esalen, many of them, in a predictable rhythm of search.

Every so often a livelier breed of cat pops in. Roger is a successful special accountant; he takes odd clients in his Bay Area office — ecology groups, a hard-nosed bunch of militant civil rights lawyers, a rock-'em-and-sock-'em labor union local. Even dressed in Esalen

<63>

undress uniform (a zip-up sweat suit stretched tight over his globular torso), he has the glossy-haired air of those white-collar professionals. He waits quietly as a tax dodge until the third day of the workshop, then sits in the hot seat with assurance. Do I need to bring him to the Now? He's riveted there already. I stare until the room quiets, and raise my eyebrows at him.

ROGER. I dreamed this last night. I woke up and I felt very tight, like there were gas fumes all over and I couldn't breathe. I went around opening every window in the room. Then I went back to sleep. Then I had this dream. I dreamt I was . . . (*his full jaw reflexively ripples over the tight muscle band*)

JACK. Present tense please.

His fear flinches him away from his dream, a safe distance into the past. Experience related in the present tense has a freshness, but related in the past tense it has a fading unreality. Yet, if someone is avoiding, postponing the fullness of experience, the past tense keeps creeping in; a necessary protective device.

ROGER. (*staring into the middle of the carpet*) I'm in a room, which is like an auditorium. I'm there with my wife. And uh . . . we start . . . somehow there's a car. I'm looking for a car, it begins with. I am looking for this car. I parked a Mustang someplace near a very rough area, and as I start to look for it I find myself in this assembly room. There's a large group of people there with me and I'm watching this person that comes out, comes out and he's kind of strangely dressed and he takes this flashlight and he is jabbing it at this orchestra and they are playing music. And then I watch that for a while . . . and my wife is sitting next to me . . . and I decide that I have to find the car. So I get up and leave, and as I get up and leave everyone in the room begins to leave.

<64>

Before he leaves, besides jabbing, he starts doing . . . this orchestra leader . . . he starts doing all kinds of things with his face, contorting it. And he keeps opening his mouth very wide, over and over, very wide. Making these gestures. Then he takes the flashlight and he puts it in his mouth and then he attempts to put it on his chest. And it doesn't stick, and then he rubs it on his sweat and he puts it there and it sticks there. And we all leave.

I leave first and everybody seems to filter out. Then I start looking for the Mustang. We start looking in different streets, I'm with my wife at this point. As I'm looking we start going over a little rise and all of a sudden two cars . . . no, we find a Mustang but it's stripped. Everything off of it. No wheels or fenders or anything — it's just been stripped! I look carefully and it's not my Mustang, but I have the key to my Mustang in my hand. And I notice that the Mustang switch is going on and off, on and off. But this whole car, this one Mustang is all stripped, except for this one switch which is going on and off, and that's all that's happening with it. Just this stripped car with this one thing. (*Roger sweats. He runs his zipper down to the belly bulge — sweaty hairy flesh*)

And then I . . . we start going up a hill and all of a sudden one small car hurdles off . . . hurdles over a road. And it goes around and it sort of does a running kind of a turning, twisting thing. And out of it comes this dwarf woman with a man. This dwarf woman comes out with a gun and she starts to fire. Fires like a shotgun. And as she fires, she fires at me and I tell her quietly and kind of calm her, "That's not allowed, that's really not allowed." There's this sign there, this big sign, it has a body on it. And it says, "TRY NOT TO KILL ANYONE." There's a body lying flat, showing what not to do. It's a sign that I understand as I look at it. It's to tell people in this very rough neighborhood not to kill people. Then we go to this woman's apartment, this little dwarf woman. I notice that she has a birthmark. It's black on the left side of her face and white on the other side of her face. So the birthmark is covering one side of her face, making it very dark.

<65>

There's this man with her who remains very . . . kind of silent . . . with her the whole time. And my wife gets into a conversation at this time . . . when we go to this dwarf's apartment. And the conversation is, my wife tried to amuse her. And my wife says to her, "You must be a member of the Bolshoi Ballet." I know that my wife is just trying to amuse her. Then the dwarf says, "Yes, I am." Then my wife says this line, she says, "I have a niece who is sixteen years old and is also a member of the Bolshoi." And I wonder why my wife has lied to her. Then the little dwarf woman picks up on the lie. I feel that I'd better leave. And I leave. I leave my wife there. I go off. I start looking again for the car. For this Mustang that must be lost someplace. And I've got this key still in my hand. I come to the area of this building and I go up and it's offices. Ones that I recognize. They are changing slightly from mine. They seem to be bigger and they're remodeling it and making it larger.

There's a friend of mine in there. A lawyer I know from Oakland. He was working for this firm. And he was saying like . . . he was talking to a law clerk. And he was saying like, "This case is only worth like only fifty cents and you'll have to do it."

I get this law clerk to help me go out and find my Mustang. He gets in his car, we drive around, and look for the Mustang. We can't find it. We come back and I go up to the . . . there are very few people left in this assembly area. As I look around there, I . . . start to look and wander around. I find my stepdaughter there. She's wondering what I'm doing there. I tell her I can't find my Mustang. I keep being on one side of the city where there are circular streets, but I can't seem to get over to them. And then I start to wander over toward the hill. It starts to look like Los Angeles. All the buildings seem to look ripped off.

And I meet this woman on the street and she says, "I'm looking for this Café something," and I think she's really inviting me for something, and I know that she is. I say, "That's not really near here, it's down in Tiajuana and I don't have time to take you there. I haven't got time because I have to find this car." And I look at her very

<66>

knowingly and she says very knowingly, "All right." And then I walk up the hill. I'm still looking for the car and I seem to be going in a totally different direction. And I can't find it. I wake up then. (*softly*) That's the dream.

JACK. (*long pause*) Man! When you dream, you dream!

ROGER. I haven't had a dream in a long, long time.

JACK. All right. Is there any element of the dream that particularly interests you?

Once we lock onto the pattern, Roger's life pattern, we can unroll endlessly. I've never tried to extend a dream to its limits, but theoretically there is no end. This dream for sure could exhaust every aspect of Roger's life. So where to begin? I can't know. Let him decide, it's his dream. Only his conscious knows which gestalt is ready for closure. Listening to the dream, I feel I am examining a drawing by George Gros, the German caricaturist, or reading a novel by a middle European satirist — a vivid, grotesque, accurate picture. I make a guess that Roger must be from Hungary or Austria or somewhere around there.

ROGER. Ah yeah, the dwarf woman with the gun, and the silent man. That scene especially, with the car turning over and over.

JACK. (*to the group, pedantically*) You see, a dream like this could be an entire therapy . . . an entire personality explanation. Even a fragment of a dream can be. (*I decide against delaying Roger with more bullshit and speak to Roger*) I'd like you to have an encounter with the dwarf woman.

ROGER. (*talking to the little wire garden table opposite him*) All of a sudden I think I know who you are. I think you're my mother.

JACK. Be your mother.

<67>

Roger sits heavily on the low table, careful to stay in the secure middle.

ROGER as mother. (*decisively*) I am *mad* at you. I'm *really* mad at you. You've gone off and finally brought me to San Leandro. I spent all those years in an institution and you never came around to see me. I could kill you. (*voice is higher, a brittle whine*)

ROGER. (*smugly*) Mustn't do that. I know where I am, and I say, "Mustn't do that. Naughty, naughty!" I have the power now.

JACK. How does your voice sound to you?

ROGER. My voice?

JACK. Uh-huh.

ROGER. Like super-calm and controlled, and now I'm beyond the whole situation. I say to her, you're not lethal any more. You can't kill anybody. You can do it once to me, but you can't do it any more. I'll leave you there with the dark man, the dark, shadow figure.

JACK. What's your left leg doing?

This pattern is complicated, I go to the physical level for direction. There are a lot of gnomes, witches, and warlocks in *this* old wood-work! But remember, I'm not unraveling the complicated feelings and relationships implicit in what he says; my goal is for Roger to have an emotional experience that finishes some unfinished business for him. In accountant's language, to close the books on an old, delinquent account for him.

ROGER. Going up and down.

JACK. Ask your left leg.

ROGER. Why are you going up and down, leg? I don't understand you. I don't get any messages from you. You're just bouncing.

JACK. Let the left leg speak.

<68>

ROGER as leg. Can't do that. I won't let you. Can't get away with anything. Not a fucking thing. Don't try. I'll just pull you right back. We have our own ways of dealing with you. (*pause*)

ROGER. And then I respond, I know you have and I'm tired of it!

JACK. I'm tired of *you*.

ROGER. I'm tired of *you*! And I'm tired of your way. (*pause*)

JACK. What's happened?

ROGER. it's stopped.

JACK. Uh-huh.

Meaning, "Of course, you knothead, go right up to those fear apparitions and they kowtow like redheaded woodpeckers on a pecan tree."

ROGER. My leg's relaxed.

JACK. What does the left leg say?

ROGER as leg. OK. I'll watch you and give you a chance. (*nagging quality*)

JACK. Who's talking?

ROGER. (*sigh*) A whole orchestra of people. Children, divorced wives, or wives being divorced, fathers, sisters, friends. That's all I can think of.

Isn't that something? All these people riding on one bouncing leg, won't even let this poor fellow have a meeting with his crazy mother without nagging, "Hey, pay attention to us too!"

"And a whole orchestra of people ... " the dream orchestra with Roger the crazy conductor, and I don't pick it up! It would have been dramatic to pick this up here, to have Roger conduct his whole orchestra of people. The ghosts of his entire life would be in that orchestra. I decide, however, not to go that route. His dream material

<69>

is so extensive and diffuse that I sense I'd better not spread him out too far.

JACK. What are you experiencing now?

ROGER. Closing off.

JACK. Say to them all, "I'm closing you off again."

ROGER. I'm closing you off again.

JACK. (*pause*) How do you feel now?

ROGER. OK.

We've lost momentum. I haven't danced the right measure; he's lost the thread.

JACK. How does OK feel?

ROGER. OK feels like just like, uh, like slightly unaware, like in my head. Like if somebody would run into me I would be surprised at the force.

JACK. I want you to be the little car of your dream. The one that crashes.

ROGER. The little car. OK.

I make the connection between Roger's words, " ... run into me ... surprised at the force ... " and the little car of his dream. He throws himself into my suggestion with enthusiasm and the results are startling. He flings himself, like a bowling ball, from the chair, does an expert rolling somersault and lands on his back, legs still bent.

ROGER. Blam! Smash! Blam! (*rolls on floor*)

JACK. What does the little car say?

<70>

ROGER. Oh, I'm all smashed. The car is all smashed on the pavement.

JACK. (*loudly*) Be the car! Be the car!

ROGER. This car's smashed!

JACK. I'm smashed.

ROGER as car. I'm smashed! I'm smashed. God, I'm smashed.

JACK. Feel how you feel smashed. (*heavy breathing from Roger*) Feel it.

ROGER. (*groans*)

JACK. Say to yourself, "I've gone wild and I'm smashed.

Perhaps letting himself go, be "wild," is associated with punishment. He has punished himself by injuring his shoulder. Maybe I'm wrong, and he'll say, "That doesn't feel right."

ROGER. I've gone wild and I'm smashed.

JACK. OK.

ROGER. I'm wild and I'm smashed.

JACK. How does that feel?

ROGER. I'm sick.

JACK. Just keep saying it, "I'm out of control and I'm smashed."

ROGER. I'm out of control and I'm smashed. No, I'm in control and I'm smashed.

JACK. OK.

ROGER. I'm in super control and I'm smashed. I feel smashed, therefore I'm smashed.

JACK. How do you feel as the car?

ROGER. Hurt. Sore. Surprised. I hurt myself. See, you do that and you hurt yourself.

<71>

JACK. Who's talking?

ROGER. Me. Me soothing myself.

JACK. All right, soothe your shoulder, your hurt.

ROGER. (*softly*) Aw! Hi, Swelly!

JACK. Now say, "Mother, soothe me when I hurt." (*the hurt child wants his mother*)

ROGER. Mother, soothe me when I hurt. But she does inside.

JACK. What does the outside one, dwarf woman, say?

ROGER. You can't make contact with her. You just play games with her. She's crazy.

JACK. What does she say? Be the dwarf woman.

ROGER as dwarf woman. (*he speaks in German*)

ROGER. (*to group*) She only talks about food.

JACK. Say that to her.

ROGER. You only talk about food. (*as though talking to a pet animal*) You want a hamburger?

JACK. How do you feel now?

ROGER. So, so.

JACK. Now the shadow man. The dark man. Put the dark man there. On the pillow.

As Roger won't deal with mother, I bring in his father. Earlier the shadow man seemed to be father. So he is also Roger's dark side, his unknown self who is also feared. Physically the left side is usually the dark side. "Sinister" means left. In baseball the "lefty" has special skills that the right-handed player has to look out for; the place of honor is on the right hand, an illegitimate child is said to be "from the left side," and so forth. Very often, the left side is the mother.

<72>

ROGER. I don't want to look at you. I don't want to see you. (*frightened*) I blot you out, you son of a bitch. (*sobs*) I can never make contact with you. I just keep you a shadow figure and there you are. I don't want to see you. I can't deal with you. I can't deal with myself like you.

JACK. What?

ROGER. That's it, Jack.

JACK. That's what?

ROGER. That's who he is! He's my fucking father! You're my fucking father. (*Sobs*) Can I get rid of you?

JACK. Tell him what to do.

ROGER. (*hard, bitter, tensely leaning forward*) Keep your distance! Keep your distance! I'll keep mine. That's our bargain. (*moves to the other chair*)

ROGER as father. You've got nothing to fear at all. See, look. Nothing wrong with me. Come close. (*he speaks in a honeyed Hungarian accent*) Come close.

ROGER. (*sharply*) No! Don't come near me. I've tried. Every time I try I get smashed. I get hurt. I can't deal with you.

His father *is* Hungarian! What do you know! Roger's mother is German — and both shape his personality so his very dreams are flavored by the old country!

Roger turns and his look appeals for help.

JACK. What do you want from me? (*softly*)

ROGER. I don't know. I felt I recognized who the figures are. Maybe that's the whole point, in realizing that. I don't think I can make peace with . . .

JACK. Tell *him* that. (*again, speak to, not about. Confront, confront!*)

<73>

ROGER. I don't think I can make peace with you. I don't think I can go any further with this dream or this conversation; I don't feel I can. Nothing I can do. We're at an impasse, and it's OK. Now, I'm a father. My children, I can deal with them. Somehow, to some extent. Not too well. But I can't deal with you. You're going to die soon. Your heart's bad. It's OK.

JACK. *I'm* OK.

Emphasizing the *personal* pronoun, not the impersonal. In this therapy we keep plugging away at reclaiming as much disowned self as possible. Using the impersonal is a common way to disown feelings we're uneasy about. When I feel anger, I say, "*It* makes me mad!" Whatever "it" may be, the anger is *mine*.

ROGER. I'm OK.

JACK. Now say, "I'm not OK."

ROGER. No, I'm OK.

JACK. Say, "I'm not OK." Find out which sounds correct.

ROGER. I'm not OK. I'm not OK. I'd like to end the shadow. But it's not up to me.

JACK. It?

I'm not satisfied that Roger is OK. I state the negative so he can feel in himself which is more "him." This leads into a typical impasse; his confusion is approaching the shadow-father of his unconscious. When a person runs right head-on into the impasse his rational self is jammed. In the unconscious opposites exist rather comfortably; in the conscious they jam the computer. Gestalt therapy in one sense is just getting people into their impasse solidly, then encouraging them to stay there until the impasse vanishes as if by a miracle. I asked Fritz Perls to explain the impasse resolution. He replied, "I don't know what happens, unless you call it God's mercy." That was

<74>

the only time I ever heard Fritz speak of God with any acknowledgment or reverence.

ROGER. The moving of the shadow.

JACK. Replace "it" with "I."

ROGER. I'm not up to . . . something's wrong here.

JACK. Replace "it" with "I."

ROGER. I'm not up to I.

JACK. No, "I'm not up to me."

ROGER. I'm not up to me. It doesn't make sense, Jack.

JACK. Say that.

ROGER. I'm not up to me.

JACK. Again.

ROGER. I'm not up to me.

JACK. How do you feel about that?

ROGER. Doesn't make sense.

JACK. How do you *feel* about that?

ROGER. I don't have any feelings about it.

JACK. OK.

ROGER. I'm not up to I . . . me.

JACK. Now try, "I am . . . up to me."

ROGER. I am up to me. It doesn't make sense, Jack. I am up to me . . . I am *on* to me. Makes sense now. I am up to me. I am *up* to me. (*long pause*) I *am* up to me, nobody else!

JACK. I feel like stopping here. How do you feel?

ROGER. OK. I do too. There's lots more I'd like to know, but this is a good place to stop.

<75>

There is another long pause. I notice that Roger's breathing is becoming deeper, more even. He is visibly much more relaxed.

JACK. (*to group*) This dream is unusually detailed. I'd like to know more about the orchestra, the cars, and all that. We don't have the time and Roger doesn't have the energy. He's realized that his father isn't Big Daddy any more, that he, Roger, is his own master. He responds, is response-able to Roger. Saying, "Oh, Daddy, you're so cunning, seductive, overwhelming that I can't deal with you" just isn't reality — so now he says, "I *am* up to me." (*pause*) Enough bullshit.

ROGER. O.K. (*gets out of chair*) I sure creamed my shoulder.

JACK. Go into the sauna awhile and get someone to massage it for you. Let's take a break.

COMMENT ON ESALEN

One of the many beauties of working at the spectacularly beautiful Esalen Institute at Big Sur is the South Coast Center, which has a body-temperature swimming pool and sauna right outside the meeting room. Out the door, off with the clothes, and into the pool. And as an added enticement, the art of massage, brought to a meditational art at Esalen, is offered right by the pool in the hot sunshine.

Nudity cuts right through the concealment compulsion, the fear of self-exposure inherent in any society. I don't think nudity itself is particularly therapeutic, but nudity in a context of naturalness, as at Esalen, is another step on the road to self-discovery. In one month-long workshop I tested the usefulness of Gestalt therapy *au naturel*. In a short time nudity per se had lost its prurient appeal, what the obscenity laws call "that delicious erotic excitement." Observation of behavior and body movement in psychotherapy is fully as important as listening to words. Therefore, seeing the body without the mask of clothing can be useful. Our group met in the massage room of the

<76>

hot baths, sitting on the massage table, floor, and window sills. The nudity caused a few nervous giggles at first, then was completely accepted. I clearly observed bodily reactions I'd never known, such as changes in skin color and texture, nipple reactions (a whole treatise on nipples awaits an investigator), and much more precise observation of breathing changes with emotion. The noise of the waves below the window, the dampness and lack of comfort have discouraged repeating the experiment in the massage room, and I've not been at ease in suggesting general nudity in the usual meeting rooms, since propriety is one of my stronger behavioral guides. Nonetheless, I plan to follow up this experiment some day during an extended workshop.

<77>

7

The Beautiful Girl Who Gets Slapped

This dream has a prelude. In the prelude (or we might even call it a preliminary since there is some resemblance to a boxing match) the top dog, the dreamer, and the bottom dog, myself, come to blows. We then settle our differences, proceed with the drama of the dream itself, and finally resolve the dreamer's impasse.

I've always had difficulty saying "No" to a request for help. My father recognized this early. I was about sixteen when he said "Jack, you're lucky you weren't born a girl because you wouldn't have had a period from your first birthday to your last." So when Ruth begged me in her most touching waif-of-the-Big-Sur-Canyons manner to let her in my workshop, strictly for free, I hesitated and hesitated and finally said OK. But I held some resentment which I projected on her — to what extent you must decide from the following.

Ruth and I have worked together for years. She is unique a free childlike spirit with a wise woman's personality. She is also a supreme manipulator whenever she sees fit to manipulate. I'm on guard as she sits next to me in the hot seat, thinking, "This time

<79>

Ruthie baby, you're going to work! None of this look-at-cute-intellectually-charming-me bullshit!" So right off she starts by turning to me, joining her hands together and bowing:

RUTH. I bow to the essence in you. (*voice solemn.*)

JACK. Ruth, you're here to work, cut out that dramatic shit!

RUTH. (*innocently*) I'm only acknowledging your essence. Our essence is our link with God, that part of us unsoiled by ego. Ego is our own separate individual self that says, "I'm here and you, God, are over there."

JACK. (*Ruth is playing her own ego games in the name of essence.*) No, you don't get away with that!

RUTH. What are you going to do about it? (*pertly.*)

JACK. You said you want to bow to the essence in me?

RUTH. That was a feeling I had in me that I was trying to push down.

JACK. OK. So put that feeling over there and talk to that feeling. (*she has to look at her own behavior. Nothing I say will be convincing.*)

RUTH. (*to the chair*) You're real, and yet you're dramatic. (*loudly, forcing words out.*) I distrust that part. I distrust the drama part and I try to push you down ... (*sudden tears*) and I don't want to push you down. (*childlike.*) I've been told so many times, "don't be so dramatic." And now anything that's different, even when it's real, sometimes, you know I push it down. (*more tears.*) People won't like me. And 'cause sometimes they're as phony, I push it down, and you're real!

JACK. (*harsh voice*) Be aware of how dramatic you're being right now.

Completely unexpectedly, Ruth swings blindly and hits me with a roundhouse right and left. There is a uniform gasp from the group.

<80>

The microphone and tape recorder have been knocked over. I hesitate momentarily; then, with some restraint, backhand her along the side of her head, firmly but without damage. She springs from her chair and runs to the center of the room, then turns like a cat chased by a dog. I follow and stand over her. She is afraid and defiant like a child before a parent.

JACK. Don't do that again! (*in a loud voice*.) You're phony. You're phony! Now sit down over there. (*long pause*)

Ruth yields, turns and goes to the hot seat. I follow and sit next to her. I'm reflecting on the pros and cons of slapping women in workshops, a chancy business. With Ruth I'm not concerned; we are friends and have worked together for three years. My response to her violence is both spontaneous and controlled. A friend did the same thing in a weekend workshop and has a million-dollar damage-to-dignity and malpractice suit on his hands. This was in my mind before slapping her — but no, Ruth must be treated directly, as an equal, not with therapeutic restraint — so, *pow!*

For me to guide Ruth along the blind paths of her unconscious, I've got to be in charge. She must know I'm in charge so that when I spot her distracting herself from her goal of self- discovery I can step in and stop her. Now you and I and Ruth all know that I, Jack, am *not* in charge, that God is directing Ruth and me as far as our egos will permit. Nonetheless, Ruth at this point needs me to say, "Cut it out, baby, you're playing games!" You might object that 180-pound me invoking the name of God to justify slugging 105-pound Ruth is at best making feeble excuses and at worst sacrilegious. Well, love is not always a powderpuff kiss. I *do* put the interest of Ruth first.

Is my action in Ruth's best interest? There's no way to know. My action *feels* right. And, following this little slugfest, Ruth finished an important gestalt and became more mature. I made my choice to slap her as quickly and as deliberately as a surgeon looking down on a life-or-death choice, with no guarantee on any action.

<81>

Would I always respond so? Of course not. Some women I wouldn't lay a gnat's eyelash on. Some I might kiss lightly. Some I would throw out of my workshop or just stop work on at that point. No rules, no guidelines, except love and responding to where the person is at. That is being response-able.

The group is amazed at this interchange except for the old-time encounter groupers. They've seen more violent nights. One man, however, tells me that he was on the point of jumping up and protecting Ruth from my masculine violence. I laugh. He is annoyed.

RUTH. (*breathing heavily and sniffing*) I see myself empty. OK, now what do I do, tell me what'll I do ... (*she speaks with a childlike precision*) there's nobody around. Everything's empty. There's a path. It's like the old path used to be, down to the paths. (*she's referring to Esalen Hot Springs*) Only this path goes up. I see these feet, they're my feet. I feel all the muscles. And my eyes look down and it's like dim light coming from my eyes. And cold. Each foot is in a cone of light ... (*sobbing*) going up the path ... and the rocks, and they hurt. And I keep moving my feet up the path. And I keep moving my feet up the path. And I can't see anything but these feet and part of the path. I make myself be careful, and I (*sigh*) wake up (*sigh*). And I lie there and I think and (*pause*) and I go back to sleep.

I find that I'm still there. And I want to see something around. I want to see bushes, and trees, and (*breaks into sobs*.) I want to see where the end is, just something and ... and there are white letters in the light and they say in Latin, "Sum, ergo amo [I am, therefore I love]." Then I wake up, no I ... ? ... when I see that. And I get a feeling of ... ? ... and then I wake up. And ... I don't know. Yeah, I feel OK, but I didn't want to tell myself that's who I am. I am, therefore I love.

JACK. Speak to the path, Ruth. Speak to your path.

<82>

The path in Ruth's dream is obstructed by Ruth's own ego. The ego is inwardly blind, outwardly pseudocompetent, and always confused. Ego always hurts us in the end. It leads us by the brightest, smoothest, most socially approved freeways into the most horrible situations. Although our inner path (our essence) is narrow and often dark and difficult, it is the only truly self-rewarding path. Ruth's dream is what I refer to as an *essence dream*. Ruth is close to the true essence of herself most all the time whether dreaming or awake. She is one of the very few people I know who is actually living out their dreams. Ruth is freely one of God's children.

Here in her dream Ruth is close to a fuller realization of herself. She is aware, in the dream, of the cloudiness of her own ego, aware that her true path is difficult, and aware that she cannot see the end of that path. I yearn for her to *discover for herself* that there is no end; that the path never ends for any of us, not in this material life. Each moment is now, the beginning *and* the end. A unique completeness unto itself. Each moment, to a truly free spirit, feels just like Christmas morning to a five-year-old kid. Ruth, I know, is capable of this.

RUTH. (*in a wail*) How long are you? How long are you? I don't mind that you have rocks and I don't mind the dirt, and all the dust, I'd just like to know how much longer. (*sobs*) You're so narrow, I can't see anything but you and my feet. There's so much more, I know. I'm trying, I know there are people, I want to see people. (*sobs loudly*)

JACK. Come on over here and be the path. Be Ruth's path.

RUTH. (*no longer crying, softly and sadly*) I'm dusty and I'm stones, and I cut your feet. I don't know where I end either. I'm only alive when your feet are on me. They feel good ... stepping. I want your company. I'm sorry I cut you. (*pause*) I'm tired too. I don't want to hurt you. (*long pause*) I'm so tired ... open up, please. Oh please open up. I'm tired. Please open for me! Please open for me, please! (*sobs*) I want you. (*sobbing stops, voice changes*) It's not time yet!

<83>

JACK. Who's talking?

RUTH. I am — Ruth.

JACK. Let the path reply.

RUTH. I'm a path, I'm not a grave . . . you will yourself on me even can will yourself into the grave too. It's up to you. I'd rather you stayed with me.

JACK. Whew . . .

RUTH. Me too!

JACK. All right, come sit up here in the chair again. Now this is your dream, you can do anything you want with it. So I'd like you to continue the dream and finish it. Complete the dream any way you want to. In other words, go back . . . finish the dream.

RUTH. (*Alternates between little child voice and more mature voice.*) People, lots of people. My friend is there. (*Sobs*) I want a path beside them. (*child's voice*) The people together. Mostly they're little bats. Lots of company. (*laughs*) I've lost company but I'm not going to be alone. (*voice gains resolve, purpose*) Walking past them takes so much. All right, I'll get energy from someone in my dream. All right, I have energy. I've got more energy than is required to walk the path . . . (*pause*) Anybody help? Will anybody help? OK. That's enough; just to walk holding hands.

JACK. Who are you holding hands with?

RUTH. (*childish voice*) The man, the person over here closest to the path, he's holding my hand. And the person over here, we held hands, and . . . and the person next to this one held hands. And everybody started holding hands. (*sobs. I take her hand, give my free hand to next person; the entire group becomes a circle*) Oh, I just keep forgetting. (*sobs*) Oh, I'm so *tired*. Oh, wow!

JACK. OK. One more thing. I want you to say, "Jack, I'm dramatic and I'm beautiful."

RUTH. Jack, I'm dramatic by God, and I'm fucking beautiful too!

<84>

JACK. Now tell the group that.

RUTH. I'm dramatic and I'm beautiful. I'm a beautiful nut.

JACK. Now tell Ruth that.

RUTH. Ah, Ruth, God love you. And Ruth, God love you, and Ruth, God love you, and Ruth, and Ruth, and Ruth. Hey's that's nice. OK!

JACK. OK!

COMMENTS ON RUTH'S DREAMWORK

By staying with her feelings, by experiencing and not running away from her desolation, Ruth broke through the death layer into life. She has arrived from death and aloneness to life and companionship. The company of the blessed in Beatrice's vision (see "The Descent of the Holy Spirit") comes to mind.

In Gestalt terms, Ruth has experienced an impasse (her fear and confusion over the path), integrated that fear with her drive and impulses, and finally made contact with the life around her. She has enriched her personality and freed previously blocked energy. In other terms, Ruth's faith has overcome her fear, conquered her ego, and released the essence of joy and love.

With the smog of her ego-fear cleared, will Ruth have no more troubles? We know better than that. As long as Ruth has attachments, as long as she is open to the experience of living, she will be open to pain as well as joy. In life, there must be valleys or there would be no mountains. Without downs, there would be no ups.

<85>

8

The Sadistic Boy-Father
and His Daughter's Nightmare

Marchand has a daughter, Corliss. Corliss lives with Tessie, who is Marchand's ex-wife-to-be. Corliss is caught in the middle of the separation struggle between her mother and father. That is a struggle which many of us know so well. All the horrors and atrocities of civil war are acted out in family miniature.

Corliss has a dream, a nightmare. She told the nightmare to Marchand and he asks to work on the dream, believing that the nightmare of his daughter is related to his own struggles. I agree to the experiment. The dream work takes place in my Tuesday night Gestalt group. The group has become a working entity, in which most of the people are secure enough to express their involvement with the individual who is working. For this reason, the dream work is a unique combination of individual and group gestalts.

A note on Gestalt groups: I agree with Fritz Perls that group therapy using Gestalt methods has theoretically made individual therapy obsolescent, if not obsolete. Operationally, in the private practice of solo psychotherapy, the greatest demand is for individual

<87>

hours. By providing a mixture of individual, group, and three-to-six-day residential workshops, nearly any type of middle-class problem can be reasonably well handled.

As I love informality and my own comfort, the group meets on the cushions and chairs of my own living room.

MARCHAND. Corliss is seven years old. She dictated the dream to me. She dictates letters and is used to it. This is the dream: "My mother is calling my Dad. Then my Dad wanted to tell my mother something. Then my mother started screaming. Then my friend was giving me a gun. Then when I was tired of hearing my mother scream, I killed my mother. Then my stepfather called my Daddy, and my Daddy started talking. Then Harry [stepfather] started screaming as loud as he could. Then I got tired of reading my book and I standed up and said `I am going to kill you.' Harry said, `You just try.' I tried but I couldn't kill my stepfather at first. Then I shot him in the head and he fell. I remember that Lillian, Sally, and Bobby [Harry's children] were going to sleep over, but then they came and saw him on the floor and they said, `Why did you kill our Daddy?' And I said, `Because he was making so much noise on the telephone, and I could not stand it.' Lillian and Sally said, `We will kill *you*.' I got very scared and they killed me when I turned to run. Then my beloved Daddy came and got so mad he killed Lillian and Sally, but he did not kill Bobby because he was very friendly and that was that."

JACK. What are you experiencing?

MARCHAND. Well, I feel kind of good that I came here and killed the two children; like Sir Galahad comes and does justice. (*his voice is happy, delighted*)

JACK. Will you please be Sir Galahad then? Doing justice . . .

MARCHAND. You mean, kill the children? (*voice suddenly older and sober*) I can't do *that*.

Marchand has happily entered into Corliss's dream to fulfill his own inner child's needs. He and Corliss are allies against the

<88>

unrewarding adult world of Tessie. My suggestion that the fantasy be given reality through being acted out makes him suddenly aware of the possible cost in psychic pain, and he becomes conscious of his vulnerability and weakness. The willingness to experience pain is a prerequisite for maturity.

JACK. Oh? What's your objection to killing the children?

MARCHAND. I, I can't do that, I can't really kill them, I don't want to do that. (*flustered*)

JACK. OK, get up, be Sir Galahad, and tell the children that.

MARCHAND. Kill the children?

WOMAN'S VOICE. *Tell* them.

MARCHAND. Oh, what am I doing?

ANOTHER FEMININE VOICE. You're not listening . . .

Marchand begins to confuse himself with the fears of giving any reality to his fantasies. To escape he then "loses his ears," can't hear words. However, he can speak because he has the (erroneous) notion that words can't be held responsible like physical acts can.

MARCHAND as Sir Galahad. Tell the children I can't kill them? OK. You see, you just got into this mess because your father is a real prick. A slovenly, slimy asshole and it's not your fault that he's your father. You were just born into it. OK? I can't let you get away with killing Corliss, so I'm going to perform a lobotomy on both of you so that you can live (*fakes jabbing gesture toward children*) but you won't have any brains.

JACK. Now be the children and reply.

MARCHAND as children. She killed our Daddy, and he's the only Daddy we have, and you've got nothing to do with it because she

<89>

started the whole thing. So you just get out of here because you're nuts anyway because you see a psychiatrist.

JACK. *That's* prima facie evidence. Now, would you please be Marchand and reply.

MARCHAND. I really don't want to kill you, see, but I can't let you go around unharmed because you killed my only child, my daughter. So I'll give you the choice: either I do a lobotomy on both of you or I amputate one arm on both of you, whichever arm you write with.

MARCHAND as children. We don't have to sit here and talk with you. We're going to call the police, so you just go fuck yourself.

MARCHAND as himself. Then run away, out the door.

JACK. What does Sir Galahad do?

MARCHAND. I'm just sitting here. I don't feel like going and chasing them. I was just talking. I don't feel like hurting them.

Since Marchand fails at the action level he has retreated to a safe oral and anal sadistic level. But when the sadism requires acting out — actually following through on the threatened lobotomy or amputation — he is defeated by the innocent logic of the children and reduced once again to impotence, an inability to act. "I'm just sitting here . . . I don't feel like hurting them."

JACK. What are you experiencing now?

MARCHAND. I'm confused. I feel like I *should* kill them to be the shining knight and on the other hand I don't want to kill them. I just don't want to kill them.

He is stuck now in the position of reevaluating his entire basis for social control, of deciding whether he should abandon his inner guides ("I don't *feel* like hurting them") for the outer directors ("I *should* kill them to be the shining knight"). The shining knight, of course, gets the mother's loving approval — not the same as

<90>

"approving love" at all. Approving love is unconditional while loving approval is conditional. As Marchand experiences the internal influence of his mother, I conjecture, he experiences her love only if he acts in a manner acceptable to her standards. Whether or not Marchand's actual mother is truly this way, I do not know, but I would bet on my guess being accurate.

JACK. Now I'm going to appoint a jury and the jury consists of the dead people lying on the floor. Be in succession the members of the jury and let them decide what should be done.

To give him some reliable feedback, to replace the past bullshit he just tossed over the side, I let the people he's hurt most talk to him.

MARCHAND. OK. Well I'll take Tessie first. (*sits down, grunting slightly*)

JACK. So you're dead.

MARCHAND. But she's talking, isn't she?

JACK. But people don't sit up?

MARCHAND. You mean she's lying down ... And talking while she's dead?

JACK. Well, I don't know. (*Marchand lies down*)

MARCHAND as Tessie. (*voice angry*) You are the most selfish bastard I ever met in my life. You just don't care about anything but yourself. You are so stubborn, so self-centered, you are just a typical Scorpio bastard! Your land — that's all you ever think about! You don't think about other people. And you *drive* me crazy — I'm not hysterical *all* the time. It's just that you *drive* me crazy; you torture me and then, then you ... *make* me scream at you. So I think you ought to be put to death because I don't want you to be Corliss's father ... and I will get justice because my spirit is still alive, and I will get you any way I can.

<91>

JACK. And now, will you be the next juror?

MARCHAND as Harry. You know something, Marchand, you are just a punk. You don't even know what the hell you are all about. I could tell you how to run your life so easily, but you think you are *so* great! You don't know what it is to be a man. You just want everything your way. You spend your time trying to *impress* others. And I think you ought to be put out of your misery before you affect any other people. You are behind this whole thing. You had her kill us by remote control. (*laughter from audience*) You just influence her mind all the time. You poisoned her against us. You don't even work; you're not even responsible. You don't carry your responsibilities. All you think about is Marchand. And I was trying to build a good life for Tessie and I was taking care of Corliss and you come along and just shatter it all. So I, I am going to dedicate my life as a ghost to getting even with you. I'll get you. You're going to suffer for it!

Just notice how different Tessie is from Harry. The words are different, sentence structure is different, cadence is different. Tessie is hysterical; Harry is paranoid. Just amazing and beautiful, how the image of every person we meet is imprinted in our own flesh! Really, if we can't love our brother, we can't love ourselves, for our brother is inside, not outside us. Unfortunately, Marchand cannot "hear" his "own" words. These startlingly accurate statements by Harry and Tessie coming from Marchand's own mouth are within him but not yet integrated by him. As Harry says, Marchand has been spending his time impressing others, and up until a year ago when he had a nervous breakdown, never followed his own path. Now he is groping, stumbling, feeling his way.

JACK. What are you experiencing now?

MARCHAND. I don't know — as whom?

JACK. I don't know — whoever is on the floor.

<92>

MARCHAND. (*sigh*) . . . Just a waste, just a waste of lives, pettiness. What the hell is the difference (*voice discouraged*) . . . and I'm sorry I didn't kill Tessie myself. I think it would have been worth it . . .

JACK. Tell that to Tessie.

MARCHAND. It would have been worth whatever followed just to have dismembered you, to see the blood flow, and just *slash* you to pieces. And have you screaming while I am choking you to death and to have you see you are going to die and you can't do anything about it. And just to see your miserable body like the stinking carrion it is. (*From the audience, a woman's voice, incredulous: "My God!"*) Just to grind, grind it up in the garbage disposal and flush it down the toilet, where it belongs.

JACK. (*interrupting*) How old do you feel right now?

MARCHAND. (*sheepish and embarrassed*) About sixteen.

JACK. All right, be sixteen and talk to your mother.

Marchand is really down. He feels trapped, just as he did at sixteen, and goes off into violence, the refuge of the impotent. The energy he is directing toward a secondary target, his wife, is refocused by me on the primary one, his mother. Notice that in this first long speech he is obsessed with his own impotence. "Fuck you, fuck you. I don't know how to get mad at you. Fuck you!"

MARCHAND. (*reluctant*) Talk to my mother? (*stutters*) I don't have anything to say to you, mother, because you just want to be .. . I can't talk to you, just leave me alone! You're always bugging me about something. You make me act like a good boy all the time when I really hate your guts. I can't scream at you like I want to scream at you. I want to tell you that you are full of *shit*. (*tone rising and hateful*) I want to say "FUCK OFF!" and I keep on saying (*sweetly and obsequiously*), "Yes, mother I'll *do* it." And all that CRAP! FUCK

<93>

YOU! That's what I *want* to tell you. FUCK YOU! FUCK YOU! And I just don't know how to get mad at you. FUCK YOU! I just don't know how to say it.

JACK. What did you just say?

MARCHAND. (*voice back to the half-amused, half-defensive tone characteristic of him*) I just said it, but . . . that's what drives me crazy. (*his characteristic voice is his* mother's *voice*)

JACK. Tell *her*.

MARCHAND. You drive me crazy because you make me act the way you act. You know, you never *say* anything bad, and you know you, you (*spluttering*) I wish to hell you knew how to fight. I wish you knew how to swear . . . you have taken the nails out of my fingers. You've taken the teeth out of my mouth. I just can't bite. I can't hit. (*voice becomes monotonous as he relates the litany of castration*) You know I just get mad, I just start stewing inside. It drives me mad, drives me crazy. Like to kill you too, because you're a stinking hulk, a self-anointed God. You know, you're just full of shit. You're about five years old mentally and you think you're great. You drive everybody nuts. You drive father crazy. Yeah! Nothing's good enough for you!

JACK. Try this. "You're responsible for all my troubles." (*I'm trying to see if there is any limit to his ability to project blame*)

MARCHAND. You're responsible for all my troubles. That's true. You are. You really fucked my mind up. Royally. I didn't know any better. I didn't know you were full of shit. All those years and you got into my head so all I can do is *kill* you.

JACK. Sometimes I think you would have been better off if you hadn't read *Portnoy's Complaint*.

Marchand is attracting my own hostility. Perhaps I am goading him to get some self-maintaining response, some strength. Or, perhaps I just can't resist taking a poke at him. Maybe I am

<94>

grandstanding for the audience, something I smell hinted at in other work this evening.

MARCHAND. (*defensive*) I felt that way before I read it.

ANNA LISE. So it didn't make any difference?

MARCHAND. What gets me mad is, when I want to tell Tessie, "FUCK YOU!" and slam the phone down, which I can do some of the time, I *can't* you know, I try to get, y'know . . . I feel good and this guy Harry, I've told him to fuck off a couple of times and it just felt *great*. But today I somehow didn't get it all out. He just wanted to start a fight. (*pseudothreatening*) "You just better get your things out of here! You think you're some kind of shit." I didn't say anything. I just walked out, but I felt like killing him!

JACK. And what did you do?

MARCHAND. I thought as I was driving down here of picking up the phone and saying "You know, Harry, I forgot to tell you *'Fuck off, you bastard and go to hell!'*" and slamming the phone down!

ANNA LISE. It's too late, one minute too late. (*dryly, like a teacher*)

MARCHAND. (*amused, pleased with himself*) But I said, "Look, Marchand, calm down, wait until tomorrow, you're going to hurt yourself. Let him think he's on good terms with you. Then you can fuck him even better, y'see." (*tone of street corner crony giving advice*)

JACK. (*wearily*) OK. You're stuck. You're stuck right in the middle of your neurosis. But it's more of a game playing. More bullshit than anything else.

MARCHAND. (*subdued*) Where's my neurosis?

JACK. Your neurosis is that you still think other people are responsible for your welfare, your well-being. Your *mother, Harry, Tessie*, your *daughter*. All of these people are the people that decide where Marchand is at.

MARCHAND. Yeah, I shouldn't care anyway.

<95>

JACK. It isn't should or shouldn't. That's where you are. *You have given them your power.* You manipulate, get around them, you sneak out of Tessie's apartment. You do very well for yourself on the material level, but on the emotional level you still give them the power to fuck you up. The reason for this is that if you take the responsibility for your emotional welfare yourself, then you can't be a child. Understand — being a child is OK. You are so much better off than you were last summer that it's cool.

MARCHAND. What should I do?

JACK. (*impatient*) I'm not going to tell you what to do, but a lot of people here will, I'm sure. Would you go around and ask each one, please, what should I do?

MARCHAND. Joan, what should I do?

JOAN. (*pause; voices urge her, "Come on, Joan." "Spontaneous answer, Joan."*) Hmmm. My spontaneous reaction is that I'm a little bit in the same situation. (*laughter. "Beautiful." "Right on, Joan." "Takes one to know one."*)

MARCHAND. Larry?

LARRY. I don't think you *should* do anything. You *may* do whatever you want to do. Now that's you may wallow in your pity, put all the shit off on other people, that's not going to do any good for you ... that's what Jack was talking about. Maybe he was talking to me, too. But I maybe have become more aware of it. I've become more aware and so I have choices. I don't have to keep laying trips on other people and all that crap. I say do I *want* to do. Realizing I don't *have* to do anything. I *can* just wallow around in my self-pity if that's my choice.

Whew! Larry not only does the required exercises well, he does the freestyle with flair. Exactly the right answer!

MARCHAND. (*quieter, subdued*) Deanna?

<96>

DEANNA. I have nothing to tell you what to do. Do what you have to do.

MARCHAND. What would you do?

DEANNA. I don't know. I just realized I've been doing the same thing too ... laying everything on my husband.

MARCHAND. Well, that's different. Ann, what should I do?

ANN. I think it would be kind of nice to experiment with standing on your head.

Bless her! No verbal bullshit!

MARCHAND. What?!

ANN. Well, you asked me.

MARCHAND. Now? (*dismisses suggestion*) Jeannine? (*voices: "Aren't you going to do it?" "come on," coaxing*) OK. (*proceeds to try standing on head, but repeatedly falls on top of various women who are sitting on the floor*) Ouch, that hurt my neck.

WOMAN'S VOICE who coaxed him. Now you have a stiff neck and can blame it all on us.

OTHER WOMAN'S VOICE. Blame it on *Ann. She* made you do it.

JEANNINE. (*concerned*) Did you twist your neck?

MARCHAND. No. Jeannine, what should I do?

JEANNINE. I guess, pursue your transcendental meditation. I find it helps me a lot.

MARCHAND. (*loftly*) OK. Jane?

JANE. I don't think I have any suggestions. I guess you'll just have to fight it out with yourself.

MARCHAND. Paul?

PAUL. Just be Marchand.

<97>

MARCHAND. Anna Lise?

ANNA LISE. Well, it struck me, if I were you, I'd stay away from that house. If I were to have my daughter with me, I'd have her brought to me. Then you could stay out of that type of trouble. You are asking for it by going to the house.

MARCHAND. Well, it was a birthday party, today. My daughter's party.

ANNA LISE. Well, I didn't get that. But still, don't even go to that.

MARCHAND. Lyn? Is that your name, Lyn?

LYN. Yes. I don't know what you *should* do. My fantasy about what you *will* do is that you will go on wallowing in it and wallowing in it until you're bloody sick of it, *then* you'll do something else. That's what *I* generally do.

MARCHAND. (*pause ... softly*) OK ...

JACK. (*inquiring*) OK?

MARCHAND. Yes. Thank you.

JACK. Thank *you*.

LARRY. I wonder why you didn't ask Jack.

MARCHAND. I *know* what Jack would say. (*voices: "Oh?"*) OK, what do you say, Jack?

JACK. You be Jack. What does Jack say?

MARCHAND as Jack. Look, Marchand, you know what the choices are. You determine your own fate. If you want to be a victim, you'll be a victim. If you're ready not to be, you won't be. You make your own choices.

MAN'S VOICE. You read minds too.

MARCHAND. Jack, what were you going to say?

JACK. Nothing nearly as nice as *that*. (*laughter from group*) It's like I was thinking about my own experience in the Arica training. I

<98>

realize that I haven't really learned one intellectual general principal for a better way of doing things. I've really made about every mistake I could make. The only difference I can see now is that I seem to learn more quickly. I process my mistakes more quickly, so that when I learn something, I *know* it. I *did* it, I have no abstract principle for a guide. Simply, that having fucked up in about every way I can fuck up, I've learned a bit how not to. And there's a little evidence that I don't have to make the same mistakes over and over again so many times. Marchand, I think you're learning the same way. Hopefully, you'll find ways to learn more quickly . . . At the same time, unfortunately, you're passing your karma (residual unfinished business in the form of character structure, neurotic symptoms, blocks, and the like) along to your kids, just as your parents passed their karma along to you. That's the way of the world.

COMMENTARY

Marchand is operating during this dream work very much the way he operates through most of his life — in the guesswork, game-playing, and neurotic level. He does break through occasionally into some sort of honest emotion, but the anger and sadism that come spilling out frighten him, and, giving in to his conventional codes, he withdraws again to the world of words and games. He is in the same boat as most of us (maybe 50 percent of the population of this country).

Yes, he is in trouble. Staying a child so much of the time is difficult. Children *are* vulnerable; fears *are* overwhelming; the world *is* a wide and lonely place. Since Marchand's developmental skill in coping with the world has been retarded, he is struggling along with tools that are ill-suited to the task of adult living.

I do admire his tenacity and his search for his own basic reality, the truth about himself. The search, of course, is a search for survival. Truth (about yourself and your relation to the world) *will* really set you free as the New Testament says; it will enable you to

<99>

survive and to live without the burdens of false images. As long as Marchand continues to search with the determination he has shown, I must remain optimistic about him.

In this particular dreamwork, nothing dramatic develops. There is no great breakthrough. There is, however, a bit more of Marchand that is revealed to Marchand. Another little trickle of truth. In this way, the session is of value to him. Slow, plodding, but some progress. I hope he makes it.

<100>

9

A Poetic Nightmare

Perry is a member of our Tuesday night Gestalt group along with
Marchand (see " . . . His Daughter's Nightmare"). He asks to work
on a poem he has written. I'm stretching some points to include this
poem in a book on dreams. But there is a similarity between poems
and dreams. Both are fantasy in which unconscious factors come
close to the intellectual surface. Besides, I like this poem. I can stay
with Perry and feel along with him much of what he is feeling. I can,
along with the poet, get out of my fearful clinging to the past. I can
step on this earth, in this time, and really love *it*. The dream is ours
and we are awake.

PERRY. This is a poetic nightmare, or a nightmare poem, I'm not
sure which. (*pause while he shuffles through mimeo'd copies of his
poetry*) It's called "Nightmare."

Stand up now,
there's no use sleeping,
waiting for the maybes of promises,

<101>

I cannot have the love I never had,
hoping for wombs of the past to give birth to
feelings I never felt.
Words never spoken, some days that never dawn.
Kisses that stayed on lips ungiven,
falling into mouths digesting what-ifs and could-have-beens.
Come with me into the Now,
Let the fantasies dreamed out of touch of Now
dissolve into the granite of the past.
I am letting go of my nightmare.
It is over.
Let me hold your hand for a moment to steady my first steps.
The dream is ours, I am awake.
I am kissing you Now and
it is beautiful

I think I am feeling like Marchand. I'm stuck. I thought I'd given up the past and ah, the last few days I've gotten back in, starting blaming. What if things had been different, and all that shit. In a way I don't know where I'm at. (*voice low and discouraged*)

JACK. All right ... where's your screen of awareness, right now? Begin, "Right now, I ... " What's your awareness?

Perry starts out in the bottom dog position. Some memorable Gestalt games have resulted from accentuating the bottom dog. Here, however, I choose to turn his energy toward awareness of the Now, in place of running those old underdog tapes again. Now awareness is always a good idea and seldom fails to reap a rich harvest of increased reality contact, which, plowed under, gives a good soil for returning to the unfinished business.

PERRY. Right now, I'm aware of the group. Right now, I'm aware I'm resisting wanting to talk about money. Right now I'm aware I'm

<102>

wishing I'd not said anything. right now I'm aware of wanting to hold on, not let go. Right now I'm aware of the rug, of Joan's foot, of the room. (*voice sinking quieter and quieter*) Right now I'm aware of the birds singing outside. Right now I'm aware of my anger at myself for my ambivalence, my namby-pambyness . . .

JACK. Right now my impression is that you are abstracting and generalizing. That outside of your present awareness are the specifics of your experience. So, right now I want you to change to "Right now I'm avoiding . . . " Become aware of what you are avoiding.

We are working for a reality experience. Reason is from the mind and not from reality. Perry remains aloof by generalizing. So, I frustrate this by my demand that he become aware of what he is avoiding.

PERRY. Right now I'm avoiding dealing with my anger toward Jane. Right now I'm avoiding dealing with my anger toward myself . . . Right now I'm aware of avoiding being aware. I feel like I can't get a hold of it. I won't get a hold of it.

JACK. It?

PERRY. I won't get a hold of . . . what's happening. (*someone yawns*)

I feel a remarkable boredom, indifference. The group shows about as much excitement as a bus terminal at 3 A.M.

JACK. What's happening?

PERRY. I'm just feeling a tremendous resistance to working.

JACK. Where do you experience your resistance?

PERRY. Sort of . . . in my stomach, a feeling of nothingness, of nothing happening, of emptiness in the lower part of my stomach.

<103>

There he goes, right down the drain. He clamped such a tight hold on his energy, his responsiveness, that there's nobody at home, at all. Curious thing, the way he drained the life, the interest, out of me and the entire group. We lasted as long as a thirsty horse and a gallon bucket of water. However, short of going unconscious or up-front psychotic, few people can do the energy-swallowing trick for long without getting a psychic bellyache. "Lack guts" is an admirable colloquialism; people who lack guts usually feel empty.

JACK. Well, if you're empty down there, you must "lack guts." Hmmm?

PERRY. Yes.

JACK. Then you are aware of your own cowardice?

PERRY. I become aware of my namby-pambyness, my indecisiveness, blaming everyone else . . .

JACK. Would you please, then, start playing your blaming game. Go around the group. Start out with me. "Jack, I blame you for . . . "

PERRY. Jack, I blame you for not helping me more. You've been gone several nights. Lyn, this is only the second time, I can't blame her for much . . .

JACK. What are you avoiding?

PERRY. Blaming Lyn.

JACK. Oh? (*pause*) . . . Get down to that second or third level of blaming where you get over being "reasonable" and get down to real *blaming*.

PERRY. Yeah, I want to come back to you, I'm avoiding something. I want to blame you, Jack, for not pinning me down about paying. I've not paid the last three times I've been here. That's my game, part of my game . . . ah . . . I blame you.

JACK. You're trying to blame me, but are you?

<104>

PERRY. No, I'm blaming myself. (*voice indecisive*)

JACK. You're being namby-pamby again.

PERRY. I would like . . .

JACK. Try this: "Jack, you're responsible for seeing that I pay."

PERRY. (*rushing words together, tone of a child reciting*) Jackyou'reresponsibleforseeingthatIpayandIhavn'tpaidthelastcouple orthreetimesI'vebeenhere . . .

JACK. "So I blame you . . . "

PERRY. So, I blame you for not confronting me with that. (*voice firmer*)

JACK. Now I'm *beginning* to believe you.

Perry has been looking for clues on how to act the role of intelligent, insightful patient and get approval. He's trying out one technique after another to charm and seduce me. No wonder he's a good salesman and hates selling.

PERRY. I think what's bothering me, not having paid the last three times I've been here, plus I got my first check from my new job and I'm confronted with spreading the money out and making it last and I don't like to do that. I get frustrated, I get angry, I get namby-pamby. Money is something that's perplexed me all my life. (*tone is monotonous, boring, as if he's chewed all this over so many times there's no flavor left*)

JACK. What are you avoiding?

PERRY. Talking to you about why you didn't confront me?

JACK. My impression is that you're avoiding blaming Lyn.

MARCHAND. Yeah, you're lecturing, not talking.

PERRY. (*tone of underdog snapping back at tormentor*) *You* should be able to recognize *that*, Marchand.

<105>

JACK. Well, such a nice fellow on the surface, too.

PERRY. Ah ... I guess the thing I'm avoiding with Lyn ... I was very taken with Lyn last week when she was here.

JACK. What are you avoiding *now*?

PERRY. Telling Lyn, "You're a beautiful woman."

LYN. (*demurely*) Thank you.

MARCHAND. (*prompting, demanding tone*) *And* ...

LILLY ANN. That wasn't a blame ...

PERRY. I really don't blame her for anything. She could have rushed into my arms, but, that's another thing I blame myself for, not being more aggressive.

JACK. Try "Lyn, I blame you for not being overcome with me the first time we met."

PERRY. Oh, bullshit, that doesn't fit! (*voices: "Try it." "Say it."*) Lyn, I blame you for not being overcome with me the first time we met.

JACK. True or false?

PERRY. (*considers his answer*) False.

JACK. OK.

PERRY. Lilly Ann, I called you a couple of times about Friday night but you weren't home.

LILLY ANN. (*coldly*) I don't believe you.

PERRY. Ah ... I guess I blame you for not being angry with me for not contacting you to go out.

JACK. I want you to observe how you avoid taking responsibility or your statements, how you sort of *slither* around them.

PERRY. Uh-huh ... with Marchand it's more resentment, it's envy because he's got money.

<106>

Note how Perry escapes from the reality of the unpleasantness of his actual conduct with Lilly Ann by slithering away to his abstract envy of Marchand's supposed money. Incidentally, for an interesting sidelight on group process, go through and read Lilly Ann only.

JACK. What are you avoiding?

PERRY. I didn't think I was avoiding anything. I thought I was getting right at it.

LILLY ANN. Tell *him* directly.

PERRY. Marchand: I resent you. I'm envious of your money.

MARCHAND. What money?

PERRY. You make like you're buying and selling real estate . . . (*Marchand laughs scornfully, Perry gives him the finger*) You work very hard at giving the impression you're a wheeler-dealer.

MARCHAND. Is that all?

PERRY. I grow weary. You work hard at trying to impress people.

JACK. Start out, "I blame you . . . "

PERRY. I blame you for trying to impress me.

JACK. What are you experiencing now?

PERRY. See-saw. I'm sliding back and forth . . . Paul, I blame you for not helping me more with the group. I experience that I have to work with this, especially with you.

LYN. Perry, if you would, I'd like you to make your blaming bigger, more outrageous, more unreasonable. I'd like your to blame Ann for the fact that the waiter spilled soup on your suit, you know, or blame Joanna for the fact that you had a flat tire last week . . . Just really *outrageous*.

LILLY ANN. Get out of your niceness.

PERRY. GOP, as I call Good Old Perry.

<107>

the group. I experience that I have to work with this, especially with you.

LYN. Yeah.

JACK. Act natural.

LILLY ANN. Act *un*natural.

JACK. You want to bet it's unnatural? (If advice will save Perry, he's a saint already!)

PERRY. Jane.

JANE. Here it comes. (*apprehensive*)

the group. I experience that I have to work with this, especially with you.

JOANNA. Brace yourself, darling.

PERRY. I blame you for not getting more out of the group because you don't say very much. If you'd say more, I'd say more and get more out of the group. Thelma, I blame you for not getting here sooner. (*voices: "what a gentleman. Good Old Perry."*)

LYN. Can't you find something to make Thelma responsible for?

PERRY. No!

LILLY ANN. Sweet Little Understanding Perry.

JACK. What's happening.

PERRY. I'm thinking of a girl in high school named Thelma I dug
. . .

This journey down memory lane smells more like a sock hop than reality.

JACK. I want to change the scene, please. The script changes. I wish you would place your mother in front of you and express your appreciation to her for making you such a perfect gentleman.

<108>

PERRY. (*tone full, sincere*) Mom, I want to tell you how much I appreciate your making me such a nice boy. So I call myself Good Old Perry. So I find it difficult to stand up for what is mine. I let people take things away from me. I want to tell you how much I appreciate your making me namby-pamby. How I get so uptight about not being aggressive. How I'm such a goddamn nice guy I can't have an ongoing sexual relationship with a woman. How my balls ache. I want to thank you, tell you how all that goddamn religion crapped me up. To tell you how much I appreciate your never letting Pop get close to us. And how much I appreciate your always putting him down. So it was only two or three years ago. (*tears in his voice*) that I could see how much good he had going for him. (*voice recovers calmness*) To tell you how much I appreciate all the wonderful advice and training you gave me so I seesaw back and forth. So it makes it easy not to take a stand on anything. (*voice faint*) Difficult to be angry, to express my feelings, my anger. So I analyze and try to understand things from the other person's point of view, but I don't let my feelings out.

JACK. Enough. Be your mother now. Sit over here and be your mother.

PERRY. I've done this before. (*tone of gloomy satisfaction*)

PERRY as mother. Well, Perry, you know I did it for your sake. I've only wanted the very best for you. You know I did it for your sake. You know that. You were the baby. you were special. You're the only one that got an education. I sacrificed for you ... I only did it for your sake. If I was wrong, forgive me, I only did what I had to do.

JACK. How does your voice sound?

PERRY. Sounds like my mother's. Sounds like my own voice.

JACK. yes ... Be yourself, what do you have to say to her?

PERRY. I don't really have anything to say.

JACK. I feel like stopping here. You are stuck in your gameplaying layer, your good boy. I don't feel we'll get further now. OK?

<109>

PERRY. Of course . (*laughter*)

DISCUSSION

The horrible thing is, this *is* a nightmare. Perry is possessed by this reasonable, gentle, controlling mother image. No darkling demon could do any worse. In Perry, the self and the image are so closely locked into one that his energy is knotted and ineffectual. He lacks enough energy to project his self. This is, of course, the classical infant-mother symbiosis continuing unchanged into adulthood. A maturing individual slowly changed conceives the concept that he and mother are *not* one. Each stage of development loosens the bond, but here with Perry it continues at about the ten-year-old level. Only with the fantasied image of his father can Perry get enough energy to feel his own grief. Then the controls are reapplied.

What resulted from this fantasy work? No great thing, no break-throughs, no explosive release of life. Possibly 40 percent of dream work is like this — solid grinding away at the neurotic dualism; like a surgical procedure, carefully opening the problem, defining the structures, making the optimal approach consistent with the person's overall situation. Perry is up to line four or five of his "Nightmare," his poem: his tragedy, and his hope and map to the Now.

<110>

10

The Fearful Skier

Perpetual snow bunny that I am, I feel a shaky-legged empathy with
Bob, the Hamlet and antihero of this Vermont ski slope saga. "To ski
or not to ski," that is the question. Whether it is better to risk the
bruises and fractures of uncertain snow, or slink ignominiously into
the maternal warmth of the lodge bar. To quote Bob's dream, "It's
cold out, it's gray and it's bitter ... the slopes are icy and they're
very barren ... I don't want to ski, I don't want to take the chance.
I don't want to kill myself." Brrr. Reads like opening lines from
Melville or Camus. Well, I chill myself thinking about a choice, better
get on with the dream.

    The theme I choose to call to your attention is of the unity of mind
and body. As I think, so I am. As I am, so I think. In this dream work
Bob's fear of skiing stiffens him up muscularly and results in exactly
what he fears — clumsy, dangerous skiing. Most particularly, notice
the left-right split in all its dichotomous glory, appearing first as a
physical hand signal, then turning into more obvious struggles:
sleepy withdrawal versus energy split; reluctant skier versus erratic
skis; got to prove myself a big man versus let's play safe weak

<111>

woman; upper half versus lower half or head versus body split. We then move into certain reasons *not* to act your age. That's enough for one dream, don't you think?

BOB. A couple of weeks ago I had a dream. I thought I might forget it, and the topic seemed interesting so I typed it out.

JACK. All right. Well look, I'll tell you what I want you to do. I want you to put the typed script aside and tell the dream as though you were dreaming it right now, and then you can go back and refer to it later if you want to. OK?

BOB. OK.

The accurate repetition of a dream is not as important as the *reexperiencing* of the dream. Too often, a careful, conscientious reading is a distraction from the actual experience.

BOB. I was staying ... am staying. I'm staying in a small house in Vermont with some friends. I have a date with me. I don't remember who she is. In the morning the weather is bad — dark, drizzling. None of us seem anxious to go skiing. Instead we all go about doing odd things about the house. (*Bob's tone is low, heavy, almost without interest — something like the weather he is describing*) We all do different things. And we all go our separate ways. Then for some reason I don't know, I have to go to the ski slopes. I go to the base lodge to the bottom floor of the base lodge where they rent skis. I feel an itch to go skiing. I look outside and notice that there are people skiing. A few people. It's still sort of gray and still cold but they are skiing. Then a blaze of sunlight suddenly comes through the sky and I figure maybe it wouldn't be such a bad day after all for skiing. I speak to the husband and wife who rent skis.

JACK. Hold it. I want you to be aware of what your right arm's doing. How do you feel with your right hand? What are you doing with your right hand?

<112>

BOB. I'm holding my head with it.

JACK. How does that feel?

BOB. It . . . it feels reassuring.

JACK. Can you say, "I'm reassuring myself?"

BOB. I'm reassuring myself. I'm . . . I don't know. I think it's more like I'm making sure I'm here. Making sure that's me.

JACK. You have some doubts? What are you experiencing right now?

BOB. Yeah. I'm not sure where I am . . . Yeah . . . I'm trying to be in the dream, trying to be in the dream . . . yet I'm conscious that I'm here . . .

JACK. All right. let yourself experience that uncertainty.

BOB. (*pause . . . long sigh . . . resignedly, without conviction*) Well, I know I'm here.

JACK. Now, which side seems the more here, the left side or the right side?

BOB. The left side, yeah.

JACK. Yes. Your left side's the one that's been gesturing as you talk.

BOB. Yeah, the left side. Yeah . . . yeah . . . (*faster*) I have to close my eyes sometimes to get away from here, to get some place else. When I keep my eyes open, I'm very conscious that I'm here.

JACK. All right. Continue to tell the dream, but this time close your eyes. And as you tell it, feel your right side.

I'm assuming that Bob is avoiding something by suppressing his right awareness. By asking him to "feel" his right side I am not allowing him to get too out of touch with that awareness.

<113>

BOB. I'm in the rental shed and I ask them if they have skis for rent and they say yes and they fit me with a pair of skis. The skis fit. And I look outside — the skis fit perfectly — and I look outside and I can't make up my mind whether to go skiing or not. The sky is sunny, but the slopes are icy and they're very barren. And I see a skier come down very, very quickly at a fantastic speed, unbelievable speed. He's skiing so fast, he passes a bobsled. And I think, if he makes one false move or trips, he'll be killed. He goes whizzing right by. And then I see other skiers come down, and they're all fixed in a certain position. Some of them look like they're about to fall . . . in the process of falling. But, strangely, none of them fall. They're stationary, as though they're toy people — and they're fixed in their tracks. And they're going by at enormous speed and one move and I think they'll be killed. And it sort of . . . it frightens me. And I think, I don't want to ski. I don't want to take the chance. I don't want to kill myself. But the sun . . . the sun continues to shine. And I have a feeling that I *do* want to ski. And I can't make up my mind whether to ski or not . . . and whether to use the rental skis or go back and get my skis. Waste of time to go back to the house. And then I realize that if I ski, I don't have to ski on this slope. I can ski on another slope, a less dangerous slope and I can ski relaxed. I can ski at whatever speed I want to ski. That was the dream.

Notice that the dream work has already resulted in a partial resolution of Bob's fear dilemma. He has realized, "I can ski at whatever speed I want to ski." We tend to forget this fact sometimes: that our inner self is constantly working to resolve our dilemmas and hangups. We are maintaining ourselves through constant integrations and reintegrations, through assimilation and elimination. Consider how we physically take in food: digesting, discarding, assimilating, eliminating. In similar fashion we take in perceptions: digesting, discarding, assimilating, eliminating. Our dreams are psychic traces of this integrating process, just as our grumblings, gurglings, pissings, and shittings are evidence of the physical process. In

<114>

psychotherapy I heed gut rumbles and squeals quite as much as the most precisely articulated verbal language.

JACK. OK, what do you feel on your right side now?

BOB. I just feel it. I just ... I just try to be conscious of it, of the right side.

JACK. And on your left side?

BOB. I shut it out. (*quickly*)

JACK. Say to your left side, "I shut you out!"

BOB. (*determined*) I shut you out ... (*pause, slowly*) ... but I can't ... I do feel you ... I do feel my left side.

JACK. All right, what does your left hand reply? I notice your left hand moving. Let your left hand speak. What does it say?

BOB as left hand. You can't shut me out. I'm a part of you. (*monotone, without conviction*) I'm here ... and whatever you say, whatever you do, I'm here. I'm you.

JACK. Now how does your voice sound to you?

BOB. Uncertain.

JACK. All right.

BOB. Sort of sleepy and uncertain. And I feel that the sleepiness is, like, covering up the uncertainty. That it's deliberately sleepy to cover up any uncertainty.

JACK. Substitute "I" for "it." I am deliberately uncertain.

BOB. I am deliberately sleepy and lethargic, to cover up my indecision and my uncertainty ... about myself, and what I want to do.

JACK. All right. I'm going to put this other chair across here. Put your sleepy self, your uncertain self, in the chair and talk to Bob.

<115>

BOB as sleepy Bob. (*loud sigh*) It's comfortable to be half-awake and half-asleep and not to have to make any decisions and just be so relaxed and so sleepy and so passive (*hypnotically slow*) ... and just go along and not be responsible for any decisions. Just sort of drone away ... it's comfortable.

JACK. "I'm comfortable."

BOB as sleepy Bob. I am comfortable ... I'm also a little bothered by it.

JACK. By "me."

BOB as sleepy Bob. By me . Something is pushing me. Something is prodding me. I sort of want to wake up. I want to do something else. I can't stay asleep. I can't stay this way ... (*sigh*)

JACK. All right, now go over and be awake Bob. The right-sided Bob.

BOB as right side. (*stronger*) No, you can't. (*angry*) You can't because you're holding me down. (*determined*) You're preventing me from being alive. I can do what I want to do, but you ... you weigh me down.

JACK. Can you hear your own voice now?

BOB. It's ... I think it's a little stronger. It sounded a little stronger.

JACK. Substitute "I" for "it."

BOB as right side. I am a little stronger. (*more determined*) I know ... I know I can do what I want to do. And I know that ... (*hesitates, long pause*)

JACK. What's happening? You're going back into the sleepy side.

BOB as left side. (*gently challenges*) You're not too sure, are you? I'm still part of you. I'm still here. But I do feel a little livelier. Yeah, I think you're waking me up a little bit. But I also realize that sometimes I don't have to make decisions. I have to just do whatever

<116>

I want to do and (*slightly pouting*) I don't have to decide everything and plan everything. Part of me can be relaxed ... and there is a part of you that I do ... that I do enjoy, that I do like, that is confident.

JACK. Your voice still sounds sleepy.

BOB. (*tiredly*) Yeah.

JACK. Listen as much to the tone of your voice as well as the words.

BOB as right side. Yeah, there's something ... there's something about ... about you. You in the chair ... that I don't want to be apart from. There's something about you I like. Sometimes you overwhelm me, and I don't want that. I don't want you to overwhelm me. But sometimes you comfort me, and ... (*with more energy*) I feel an affection for you. I feel an affection for the part of me ... the part of myself that can be relaxed, that cannot make a decision, that can just say, OK, whatever happens, happens. But also, when I want to make a decision, I'll make it ... if it's necessary to make it.

JACK. Substitute "me" for "it."

BOB. If ... if it's ... if I'm necessary?

JACK. You said, I can make *it* if I want to make *it*.

BOB. I can make me if I want to make me. (*determined*) I can *be* me if I want to be *me*. And I realize that I don't have to ski any particular place. I can ski wherever I want to ski. I don't have to ski in any particular way. I don't have to ski if I don't want to ski, and I can ski if I do want to ski. I can also go back to sleep if I want to go back to sleep.

JACK. All right. Now what I'm getting the feeling is that the center of this dream is making a choice. You are faced with choices. As you've said, you can *do* fine; your question is what do you want to *be*. So *be* the skier that's schussing down the slopes.

BOB. (*with some reluctance*) At breathtaking speed?

<117>

JACK. Yeah, get up and be the skier that's schussing down the slopes.

BOB. (*nervous laughter*) I'm a terrible skier.

JACK. All right, say that

BOB. Well, I . . .

JACK. Get yourself into that old schussing posture. (*Bob stands uncertainly, knees stiff, bent forward at the waist with arms stiffly outspread*)

BOB. Here I am in the presence of skiers and I don't even remember the . . .

JACK. OK, you're going down the slopes. Repeat that. "I don't even remember."

BOB. I'm trying to envision it. I can't even feel it. I can't . . . (*pause*) . . . I know (*asserting*) I have a lot of confidence in myself I know . . . I know I'm very strong. And I know I'm very . . . I know I'm balanced. And I have quick reflexes. And I'm fairly well coordinated. I have absolutely no . . . (*short pause*) fear about myself, but it's the damn skis underneath and the ice that just . . .

To handle his fear, Bob projects on the environment: "I have absolutely no . . . *(short pause while he gulps)* fear about myself, but it's the damn skis underneath and the ice . . . "

JACK. All right, speak to the skis.

BOB. (*accusing*) You're gonna slip. You're gonna betray me. And I can't do anything about it.

JACK. About you.

BOB. About you . . . (*pause*) That's what frightens me; that I'm going to hit something. Hit a foreign object . . .

<118>

JACK. OK, now, lie down and be the skis and talk to Bob. (*Bob lies on his back, staring up blankly*)

BOB as skis. Ahh ... (*loud sighs*) well ... I' can't do anything I want to do without you. You control me. I might slip a little bit, but (*quite helplessly*) I don't want to go sliding off the mountain. I don't want to go sliding into a tree. I don't want to break. If there's ice under me and I slip, it's up to you. I depend on you ... to get me right. I depend upon you to control me. You can do it. You're quick. You're just not (*hesitant*) sure of yourself. I have that feeling: you're just not sure you know what you're doing on skis. You listen to too many instructions — too many different instructions. You try to listen to everything everybody says to you. Just ski. Just control me. You've got strong legs. I have confidence in you. You look pretty strong from here.

Those sound like great skis. I'd like a pair of those for myself. It is actually Bob's right side asserting itself here — loyal in any position. I suspect though that Bob's more timid left side will soon make its appearance again.

JACK. All right, now be Bob again.

BOB. (*sigh*) I don't know. You look comfortable down there, but I ... I'm not so sure I have that much confidence in myself. But (*voice higher with disgust*) ... what am I doing on an icy mountain — an icy, rocky mountain anyway? What am I standing here for? I don't have to go down this mountain. I'm going to ski on another mountain, full of snow. I can handle snow, I can handle certain mountains. I can't handle ice and rock. You know that's just stupidity for me to go down there. I just don't want to. No reason to ... to do that.

JACK. Your voice doesn't convince me. What does your right hand say? That sounds like what your left hand says. What does your right hand say?

<119>

BOB. (*pause*) The word coward comes up — I don't know whether it's — I can't associate it with the right hand, but it's like . . . the right hand is . . . stubborn. There's a stubbornness about the right hand. The right hand doesn't want to move.

JACK. Let the right hand say, "I am stubborn."

BOB as right hand. (*with assurance*) I am stubborn. (*slowly paced, with slight tremble*) I want to prove I can go down that mountain. (*he waves his left hand*)

BOB as left hand. (*with mild anger*) Fuck you. I want to stay in one piece. I have no desire to prove anything. All I want to do is to be peaceful and enjoy myself.

BOB as right hand. (*assertively*) I want to prove that I'm a man.

BOB as left hand. Fuck you.

BOB as right hand. I'm not afraid of anything.

BOB as left hand. Well, that's great for you. What the hell does that prove?

BOB as right hand. Yeah . . . I don't know. I don't know what it proves.

BOB as left hand. Oh come on, grow up. What the hell are you trying to prove anyway?

BOB as right hand. (*dejected*) I don't know. (*trails off*) I don't know. (*Bob's right arm,which had been rigidly accentuating his words, now falls loosely to his side*)

JACK. What are you feeling? What are you feeling in your right hand? Your right arm?

BOB. It feels looser. It feels like my hands want to come together.

JACK. All right.

BOB. And . . . and a . . . you know . . . I guess that, you know . . . it's like I feel I really want to ski. I really want to ski and really enjoy . . . (*still in awkward skiing posture*)

<120>

JACK. Did you hear your voice change right there? Up to now you've had . . . you've been real. Just now your voice changed — back to the phoniness — I don't feel you want to ski. Maybe skiing is a manly "should" not a unifying "want to." Let your hands speak . . . "we . . . " Let them speak, in unison . . . "we."

BOB. I feel like swinging them; I'm not sure where they want to go.

JACK. let them say that. "We're not sure . . . "

BOB. "We're not sure . . . where we want to go. Somehow they . . . we want to go together. (*confidently*) We want to go together. Whatever do do we want to do together. (*he swings both arms freely*)

BOB. Hey. This is fun.

Hurray. We're making progress. Right and left are on friendly terms. Let's move on to another split, top-bottom. Let's unify Bob as much as we can in this one session.

JACK. OK. Now. You notice however that all your motion is above the waist, your lower half is like a pedestal. Can you get a little motion in below the waist? (*Bob swings from hips and shoulders, bending knees rhythmically*)

BOB. That feels better . . . balanced, like this.

JACK. That's true. With your left paw on your rear.

BOB. Yeah, right. I'm not used to it, but it's like — it's like, this is where I should be.

JACK. All right. That's right. Well, now you're beginning to look like you're skiing.

BOB. Yeah, right!

JACK. OK, now, get a little bend into your legs. You're not going to be able to ski with straight legs. Yeah, get a little bend in you. You

<121>

see, you've been cut off from the lower half of your body. Which guarantees that you're going to take falls on the ski slope.

BOB. Yeah, this feels much better.

JACK. OK, now, get some bend in your legs. Sort of a little sway. That's it. That's it. Now you got it.

BOB. Yeah, that feels better.

JACK. You're still a bit stiff.

BOB. (*big sigh*) Sometimes I still have the feeling that I'm going to fall backwards.

JACK. Well, of course you are. If you're standing like that, you're going to fall backwards. (*pause; Bob's breathing heavily*) OK, now, what do your arms say no?.

BOB. We're having fun.

JACK. And what do your legs say? Let your legs speak.

BOB. We're a little unsteady ... We're a little rocky and unsteady.

JACK. What do your arms say to your legs?

BOB as arms. Yeah, I know. But I wish, ah, you weren't, because we're really enjoying ourselves. (*swings arms rhythmically*)

JACK. Yeah. That's it. Go down. That's it. Each time you swing your arms let your knees bend slightly. Da dumda daa da. Good rhythm for skiing is a waltz time, by the way, cause it's nice, low, slow ...

BOB. The legs ... the legs are saying that they're still sort of unsteady. There's still something.

JACK. Let them speak, "We are unsteady."

BOB as legs. We are unsteady. We're ... we're uncomfortable. We're trying. We'd like to ski with you. We'd like to be with you. Swing with you, but we're a little ... (*sigh*) I don't know ... (*pause*). Can't seem to get ... We used to be very, very strong. We're getting old, the legs say. We're getting old and unsteady.

<122>

JACK. OK, and what do the arms say?

BOB as arms. Oh (*sigh*) . . . dry up. Jesus. (*voice stronger with disgust*) You're still all right. I don't know what the hell is wrong with you, but you're still strong.

BOB. The arms are just having fun, they really . . . (*voice depressed again*) can't get the legs really steady. I can't . . .

JACK. Say that to your legs.

BOB. (*pause*) Now you feel steady. When I stand straight, you feel steady. When I stand straight. Well . . .

JACK. Yeah, but I want you to notice that the knees are locked. Now stand straight. Stand up straight. Now let your knees . . . unlock your knees. Get a little bit of resilience. You see, the knees are really shock absorbers, like that. Now ask your legs how they feel. Turn your left leg, your left foot in, so that your feet are parallel. There you are. Now you're parallel. Now ask your legs how they feel.

Underlying Bob's top-bottom split is his fear, the fear of getting older, weak, helpless. Bob immobilizes himself to hold the fear in. He holds himself rigidly, knees stiff, since he is unstable if he bends his knees. That instability is partly a result of his permitting his feet to turn out in a somewhat splayfooted pattern. Try it yourself; duck walk, toes out. Feel steady and secure? Also, that is a poor position to ski in. Change the foot position and find out what happens. Now, this is temporary. A permanent change would require the structural integration technique of Dr. Ida Rolf, commonly known as "Rolfing." This is a further illustration of what I meant by those "As I am, so I think" remarks. I didn't analyze or explain to Bob his insufficient support, his eroding self-confidence. No tricks, no gimmicks, Just get his legs under him.

<123>

BOB. How do you feel? Yeah, better, much better . . . much better. Sometimes . . . sometimes you don't feel like you're a part of me. But now you do. (*happily*) You feel more a part of me now.

JACK. Keep your — keep your trunk vertical. That's it. Now swing your arms. See? OK, now, then, look down that dream slope that you're going down. How do you feel now?

BOB. I feel OK. I feel . . . I feel pretty solid. I feel pretty much in control of me.

JACK. Can you hear your voice?

BOB. Ah, yeah . . . yeah I hear it . . . Yeah.

JACK. How does your voice sound to you?

BOB. Sounds OK . . . yeah.

JACK. How do you feel?

BOB. I feel . . . I feel good. I feel solid.

JACK. Say to your legs, "You feel solid."

BOB. I feel a party of you. I feel you're a part of me. I feel we're together. legs are having . . . they're having fun.

JACK. Let them speak.

BOB as legs. We're having fun. We're with you. We're all together . . . (*sighs*)

That sigh again. There's another Bob who apparently wants to speak up, who's been sighing in the background for the past ten minutes. Sounds like sleepy Bob again.

JACK. OK, now, sit back here in the green chair and speak again to sleepy Bob. What do you have to say to sleepy Bob?

BOB. I forgot that . . . I forgot . . . I can't . . . (*hesitatingly*) separate us any more. There's something I can't . . . (*with resolve*) You are me. You're part of me. We'll go to sleep later on. We'll go to

<124>

sleep tonight. I just ... I don't see ... I don't see any separation. I just don't ... I just don't. The same person is in the chair.

Sorry. Wrong number. Let's dial again. Bob's dream was skiing. So I better go back to the ski.

JACK. Now, then, imagine the skis are in the chair. What do you have to say to the skis?

BOB. (*contemplates the imaginary skis for a while*) I feel like I just want to ... (*he puts his feet up on the other chair and inserts them into the skis. He smiles*)

JACK. OK. What does that feel like?

BOB. Oh, kind of comfortable.

JACK. OK, say that to the skis, "You feel comfortable."

BOB. (*affectionately*) "You belong on my feet ... "

JACK. OK. I think that's far enough. Are you satisfied to stop here?

BOB. Yeah, I feel ... I feel more together. I guess it's ... I really felt ... a ... disconnection in my body. I really felt the disconnection and I feel it coming together. I'm trying to associate it with skiing in my mind — I'm trying to, you know — I think, maybe ... I've always had a problem skiing ... I'm not as good a skier as I am an athlete. And I've always wondered about that. Like on the ground, I'm a very good athlete, any ground activity. But when I get away from the elements I'm familiar with, somehow my — the parts of my body don't seem to coordinate with each other as well as they ...

JACK. When you're disconnected. In other activities, you're solid. On the ski slopes, you have to be in balance, and not solid. That is, you're constantly slipping. After all that's what skiing is, it's slipping. So the slipping is what makes you uneasy. Well, look, what comes out

<125>

here is the very familiar right-left, and top-bottom split. And you've resolved part of that now. But, you see, you're trying to ski with your head, instead of skiing with your ... well, really you ski with what we call the kath. You ski with your pelvis. And then your awareness goes here. This is your center of balance.

BOB. And I ... close it off.

JACK. That's right ... and my guess is, that what you're trying to do on the ski slope is to get the same sort of solidity that you feel when you lock your knees on solid ground. Of course, that's exactly the wrong thing to do skiing, because in skiing you have to let this rest on the shock absorbers of the knees. So may I suggest something the next time you ski: that you have a silent conversation with your legs before you go down the slope. And ask them what they want. Because as long as you stand in what's probably your habitual pattern, with your feet out, you are uneasy.

BOB. It's odd. I've never had trouble with my legs in any event. But I've never thought about my legs ... never thought about them. Like any sport I've ever played, anything I've ever done, my legs have been superb. They've always done instinctively — and with skiing, I guess, I had to think about my legs and I couldn't make the connection ... I couldn't make the connection.

JACK. Say that to your legs. I don't connect with you.

BOB. I don't connect with you. I feel very connected with you now though ... very connected now. I feel more confident in ... I feel a flow ... I feel energy actually flowing ... I really do ... right here.

JACK. Good. You are connected.

BOB. I feel like the flow I always had when I was a kid, my body was powerful. Full of energy.

JACK. Say this to your legs.

<126>

BOB. I feel like we're young again, you know, we just all flow together. I never sat down . . . (*fond reminiscence, throaty voice*) Remember when we were kids, we never sat down. (*laughs*). We never . . . we were always jumping up and running around . . . just . . . we loved . . . just loved to run . . .

JACK. And what do your legs say?

BOB. Yeah, they . . .

JACK. Let them speak.

BOB as legs. Yeah . . . we feel happy. We feel happy now. We feel energized and happy. I just feel energy, right here.

JACK. OK, can you feel that energy moving up in your body, as well as down? Now let your legs move.

BOB. In this part, it's moving . . . I feel it . . . moving . . . Here it's a little dimmer . . . it's . . . it's still. It's more warmth than energy. here there's movement . . . it's spreading a little . . . it seems to be moving.

JACK. *I* seem to be moving.

BOB. I seem to be moving.

JACK. You see, this . . . ours is a nonleg civilization. This is one reason in our Arica training that we have Tai Chi, African dance, and various kinds of gym. To get back into the total being. And in Gestalt we use other methods to do the same thing. As is so common today, you've been increasingly cut off from your lower half.

BOB. The mind taking over?

JACK. Yeah . . . because more and more you've been going up here (*tapping his head*).

BOB. And as we get older . . . I guess it really . . .

JACK. As *I* get older.

BOB. As I get older . . .

<127>

JACK. *I* become . . .

BOB. I become more aware that I must get by with my mind instead of my body, because my body is going to age. But it's really wrong. I'm really . . . My body is still . . . there . . . and it's still part of my mind. But this has been a conscious idea of mine, that I must depend more on my mind than on my body.

JACK. Say this to your body.

BOB. I've been neglecting you as I get older. I've been shutting you out. And it's nice to feel you again.

JACK. And what does your body say?

BOB as body. It's nice to be here. *I* am nice.

JACK. All right. Can you say to your body, "I'm not going to shut you out?"

BOB. I'm not going to shut you out.

JACK. Again.

BOB. (*more determined*) I am not going to shut you out.

JACK. I'm still not convinced.

BOB. I am not going to shut you out. What I really mean is, I will *try* not to shut you out. That's what I really mean. That's what I really want to say.

JACK. You're gonna *try*. You're not gonna *do*?

BOB. Yeah. (*laughs*)

JACK. Ask your body if it's . . .

BOB. (*with resolution*) I am aware of you and I will not shut you out.

JACK. OK, OK, I believe you.

COMMENTARY ON BOB'S DREAMWORK

<128>

Bob has closed enough gestalts, finished enough unfinished business, and faced enough of his fears so that he is in stronger contact with his body. He now feels the flow of energy that is constant and steady in every living creature — the surge of life force. Intellectually oriented for most of his adult life, Bob is still a bit too much in his head — and, sorry dear reader, but you also are a bit too much in your head. Otherwise you wouldn't be reading these yakety-yakety words of mine. You'd be out digging in your garden or playing tennis or making love. As a matter of fact, if I weren't so much in *my* head, I'd be outside this beautiful Saturday in Palo Alto doing one of those neat things myself.

<129>

11

Monique and the Prancing Monster

I find Monique an elegant but disconcerting woman. She is in her late thirties or early forties, her clothes are expensive and fashionable, her manner poised and yet a little wistful. She moves and speaks with a sophisticated grace, and when she tells me that she deals with foreign diplomats in her work at the UN, I am not surprised.

I first met Monique at the New York offices of the Arica School. She comes there seeking some new road out of her self-doubt. As we chat, she talks about a nightmare as typical of the fears and distractions which have not yielded to years of psychotherapy. Partly because I empathize with her despondency and partly because I sense a valuable dream, I offer to work with her on her nightmare.

We meet in her chic modern apartment on the fashionable East Side. Her living room is harmonious and severe. As Monique speaks I can hear the soft swish of traffic far below.

MONIQUE. OK, should I start? I had this dream a month ago, so it's not very fresh in my mind. Somebody goes out to get ... I'll tell you the most vivid parts of the dream ... I can't really remember

<131>

very well. (story-telling voice) Somebody goes out to get some bread for us. I'm with some other people. And it's a woman, an older woman, and she brings back some cheese bread. And I look at this cheese bread and it has little black — looks like insect legs ... um ... kind of squirming around the outside, as though the bug were laying down on his back below the bread. And his legs are kicking and there ... just a whole bunch of these feathery black legs kicking on this bread. And I look at it and ... ah ... it's really strange. I feel sick. It's kind of a yellow piece of bread and these black legs. And I show ... I go in somewhere and I show this bread to somebody, a man in a store. And he kind of shrugs his shoulders. And then I go out and I put the bread down and suddenly some of these legs start kind of shooting up very slowly and a kind of black feathery plume starts rising from this bread. And I think to myself, what's happening? I thought they were only insects underneath, but apparently they're something else. And this plume comes up and through the bread. And we're in a house now. And then a face and legs and a body and then this kind of creature comes up and it's got a long black plume on its head, got big brown eyes, and he's got kind of jagged teeth, short legs with claws, and a silver and blue rump, striped rump. And he kind of starts walking around and ... what I'm most in touch with is more the weirdness of this creature and the strangeness of his birth, and the ugliness of this. It's kind of disgusting as opposed to a fearful dream. It's kind of weird, disgusting ... it has an unpleasantness about it.

JACK. And that's the end of the dream?

MONIQUE. That's the end of the dream. It just kind of walks around. (*voice trails off*)

JACK. All right, have an encounter with that creature. Let's go directly to that.

MONIQUE. (*squaring shoulders, sitting proudly erect, head tilted back, proud, confident*) OK ... you're ... a ... small, but you're ugly, and you're strange. You're a very strange creature and I don't

<132>

know ... (*pause*) ... I really don't understand ... you ... I don't understand ... I don't understand how you could come out of that bread. Or what you are. You don't seem very dangerous ... you're just strange.

JACK. What are you feeling?

MONIQUE. Um ... (*pause*) a little disgusted.

JACK. Where do you feel your disgust?

MONIQUE. In my throat ... it's like, "what are you?"

JACK. Say that again.

MONIQUE. What are you? What are you doing in my life? You kind of pop out of nowhere ... out of a cheese bread.

JACK. What's the creature doing right now?

MONIQUE. Kind of prancing. You know, it's got this big black plume and it prances ... (*voice louder, increasing excitement*) and the ugliest part of you is before you were born ... the ugliest part of you with those legs, those feathery legs all over that cheese bread. Kind of a prancing monster. Just kind of prances.

JACK. All right, be the monster now.

MONIQUE as monster. Um ... (*deeper voice*) I may be a little, but ... (*with sureness*) yeah, I'm a very ... I'm a very elegant monster. I've got a big black plume and I've got a silver and blue rump ... and I'm kind of small and I've got big round brown eyes. There's an attractiveness about me ... (*inaudible mumble; voice weakens*) and I ... um ... I don't do any harm. I'm not harmful. I won't hurt you. I'm kind of an ugly ... beautiful ... kind of ugly-beautiful. Ugly black plume, kind of stands straight up and feathery. And I've got these jagged teeth ... they come out of the food (*voice almost a whisper*), they come out of the food. It's kind of strange ... (*trails off*) I'm little ... I've got claws ... and my legs ... my little legs ...

JACK. How do you feel as a monster?

<133>

MONIQUE. I feel . . . um . . . (*pause, then with sudden confidence*) proud. (*in dramatic whisper, as performing lines*) "Vice is a monster of some vital mean and has to be hated, if but to be seen. We see him too oft; the lean of his face is but to be endured and pitied and enraged." Pride is my monster . . . Pride is my monster . . . (*sigh. weary and sad*) I'm very proud and I hold my head erect. (*very softly*) But I'm ugly . . . and I (*slowly and tearfully*) just prance around. I just prance around and I hold my head up and I shake my silver and blue rump and I . . . (*pause; voice is now filled with sad awareness*) Well, it's very clear. That part of my dream. Very clear.

Monique is right. One substantial aspect of her dream is becoming very clear. Her own pride, her own "monstrous" pride, a cover for something she considers ugly, something she is deeply ashamed of. I am infected with her hopelessness and would like to examine this more fully, but right now I am conscious of the fact that I must return to San Francisco within a few weeks and will be unavailable to help Monique explore herself in great depth, so I feel it is wiser to allow her to sketch in the larger picture. Perhaps then she can find someone somehow to help her further. The older woman of her dream could be a mother figure. I introduce her.

JACK. Come back and be Monique again. Now put the older woman there.

MONIQUE. The older woman?

JACK. The one who brought you the bread.

MONIQUE. You're a . . . you're . . . you're a big woman. You're somebody's mother. One of the gang's mother . . . (*mumbles*)

JACK. I couldn't hear you.

MONIQUE. Maybe somebody . . . somebody that I'm with, you're her mother . . . and . . . um . . . you brought us this bread, this cheese bread. And it's ugly. (*accusing*) You're not taking good care of

<134>

me. You're a . . . you don't care about me. You're indifferent to me. You don't notice that my bread is all ugly creepy (*with disgust*) really creepy-crawly . . . (*pause*) It's a good thing I noticed and didn't eat any of it. Nobody offered . . . (*trails off*) You're a . . . you're kind of quiet, you don't say much. You're kind of indifferent. You're aloof. That's what you are. Aloof.

I sense that this proud, well-off woman has suffered deep loneliness and poverty as a child. An orphan? Abandoned?

JACK. What are you doing to your lip?

MONIQUE. (*slowly*) I'm . . . a . . . pulling . . . mmm . . . creasing . . . pinching . . . feeing the dryness . . . (*long pause*) Mmm.

JACK. What's happening?

MONIQUE. I don't have very much to say to this lady.

JACK. Be her and see what she has to say to you.

MONIQUE as old woman. (*clears her throat; speaks in a strong voice*) You're lucky I brought you that piece of bread . . . (*haughtily*) I mean I gave that to you. I was very generous to bring that to you. You were hungry and how was I to know it would have bugs in it. It didn't have bugs in it when I saw it . . . (*pause*) You're fortunate . . . you should be thankful . . . I hardly even know you.

JACK. Try this line: "That's all you deserve."

MONIQUE as old woman. That's all you deserve . . . (*pause*) I don't have a strong sense of . . . that . . . it's kind . . . um . . . (*voice trails off; softly with sorrow*) That's all I deserve.

JACK. All right, come back and be Monique. Now, close your eyes and let yourself go back to sometime in the past when you had the same disgusted feeling that you had in the dream. See if there's any episode when you were younger when you felt the same way.

<135>

This is a highly useful technique which we employ often in Gestalt therapy. Carry back the feeling, the experience, into the past, and allow the memory to fill itself in. Don't search, but wait, be receptive.

MONIQUE. (*pause . . . low husky voice*) I'm not finding any . . . although I feel that disgust in me. It's kind of like . . . um . . . something's going on that I don't know about. Something's happening to me and I don't know what it is. I'm not in control. Everything's going along well and suddenly I dream about a monster . . . what's going on? . . . I don't like depths. I don't like to be surprised by things in my depths. I like . . . I like things to be coming from my surface more. I don't like how it bubbles up from my depths. I like to be in control . . . (*low choked voice*) I like to be in control.

Control. The control theme. By sheer will, Monique brought herself from her poor, unloved childhood into her materially secure present. And then, for a moment, her control falters and the shut-off agony of the past comes into her conscious, into her dreams. We'll not be able to do much about modifying her rigid self-control today. Cold, icy control must have long love to melt it.

JACK. All right, ask the monster what's happening.

MONIQUE. What's happening to me? What's happening? I mean, that's . . . you're like . . . um . . . very deep fear to me . . . very deep fear . . . (*softer, fading to a whisper*) very deep . . . very, very, very deep . . . very far away . . . (*she turns her head from me, into her hands*)

JACK. Can you feel your fear? Behind the disgust is the fear?

MONIQUE. Umhm . . .

JACK. And what does the monster say?

<136>

MONIQUE as monster. (*husky, choked*) The monster says, (*slowly, sadly*) "You're all alone. You're all alone . . . you're alllll alone . . . all alone . . . all alone . . . nobody . . . nobody . . . (*tearfully*) and that's scary . . . all alone . . . alone . . . (*silence*)

Suddenly the silence is broken by the sharp shrill ringing of Monique's telephone from another room. We both laugh.

MONIQUE. Well, I'm not that all alone.

JACK. Well, that depends. Monique the professional is not alone.

MONIQUE. (*whispers thoughtfully*) Yes, right. (*telephone continues to ring*)

JACK. Do you want to stop here? I'd like to go on about another five or ten minutes.

MONIQUE. Sure. But I'd better answer the phone first . . . cause I have a foreign office representative who was supposed to be here five minutes ago.

Monique gets up and goes into another room to answer the phone. Despite the fact that I am sitting in a deep lounge chair I am conscious of feeling weary and my back aching. I ask my back, "Why the weariness?" It answers, "You've come here to help her and she can't devote one full hour to helping herself. It is her weariness, her emptiness that we feel. She's afraid that if she lets down her control, allows herself to be alone, she won't exist."

Monique finishes her telephone conversation and comes back into the room. She takes her seat.

JACK. I'd like you to have a conversation with yourself as a little girl. Put the little girl that was you there in that seat opposite and talk to her.

MONIQUE. (*contemplating*) Little girl . . . (*quick sigh, then quietly*) kind of fat and ugly . . . nebbish . . . scared . . . afraid . . . (*with*

<137>

affection) it's like you always want to do what's right. You want to figure out first what's right and do the right thing ... kind and very sensitive ... wishing that the whole world would be sensitive to you as you were to the whole world ... (*whimper*) but nobody is. Nobody ... scared ... kind of ... a nebbish ... scared and sensitive ... silly ... (*pained disgust*) awkward ... (*sympathetically*) taken advantage of ... (*trails off*) I went from there ...

JACK. "You went from there"?

MONIQUE. You went from there to street fighting ... (*sadly*) to picking on people and hurting them ...

JACK. What's your right hand doing to your left hand?

MONIQUE. It's holding, comforting, squeezing. (*tearfully whispering*) I want it to care.

JACK. What does your left hand say?

MONIQUE. Hold me tight ... It's like ... um ... this little girl ... we've gone into a lot of trips ... a lot of a ... a lot of ... um ... desperate ... seeking after love ... (*inaudible whimper*) and you were just ... (*moaned whisper*) hurt ... oh ... oh ... oh.

JACK. Can you find any love in yourself for her?

MONIQUE. (*sniffs*) More pity than anything else ... poor little girl ... tried so hard ... (*sigh, sniff*) and failed ... (*tearfully*) tried so hard.

JACK. Ask the little girl if she feels she's failed.

MONIQUE. (*husky with contempt*) That little girl doesn't know anything.

JACK. (*insistently*) Ask her.

MONIQUE. (*whisper*) Have you failed? ... (*sniff*) and she'll say ... (*little child's whimper*) I don't know ... I don't know ... I don't know what to do ... don't know how to do it ... I'm doing the wrong thing ... might be doing the wrong thing, but I don't know how to do it ... don't know how ... don't know how ... (*trails off*)

<138>

JACK. Will the grown-up Monique say, "I'll show you how"?

MONIQUE. (*adult voice*) I don't know how either. I don't know how. Abandon the search.

JACK. Have you really? (*gently*) Have you really given up?

MONIQUE. No, I . . . (*pause, sniff*) haven't given up.

JACK. You see, you can't . . . you can't *find* love. You can find romance. You can find excitement. You can find sex. Not love; love *comes* to you.

MONIQUE. What?

JACK. Well, you know . . . *pause*) yeah . . . I'm very sorry.

MONIQUE. About?

JACK. About your monster.

MONIQUE. Well, where I'm feeling to . . . is that . . . um . . . I don't know .. I mean there are people I love in my life . . . um (*slowly, sadly*) what I don't have is the love of a single person . . . who is my single person . . . and I'm his single person . . . I do have love . . . and I'm not sure that that single person exists for me. I don't know if I'm going to have a single person.

JACK. I don't know about that. But I do know that until you can love your own child, you're going to have a hard time . . . Well, I think it's probably impossible to love somebody else in the innocent fashion that you really want. And the child is your innocence. I guess we've all lost most of our innocence, but as long as we still have our child, we can remember innocence . . . Your child is still very much with you . . . (*pause*) Look . . . here's . . . I'll say it to you . . . for the first time I have a feeling of liking you . . . as apart from respect or admiration or so forth, which I've had, but I like you now. Now, if you decide you want to go further in this way and I can help you, I'll do that . . .

<139>

The ringing of the telephone interrupts and terminates our session. I excuse myself and leave for another appointment. Monique goes to answer the phone. I've not heard from Monique since that evening.

COMMENTARY

Loving myself as I was as a child is absolutely the crossroads of personality development. If I can't find love, compassion, acceptance, understanding for that early self, then I sentence myself to travel a lonely road, destination perpetual loneliness, emptiness. We are so limited in our powers as children, we are so totally at the shifting mercies of forces entirely beyond our control! As adults, we often wrap ourselves in the symbols of power, money, position, connections, and despise those persons without power; we also despise ourselves when powerless, when helpless children, we despise our inner self, our child, still present, still hungry, still suffering, still afraid. "Unless you become as a little child, you cannot enter the Kingdom of Heaven." That "little child" is *you*, your own inner self, your child.

<140>

12

The Girl in the Fellini Movie

A Japanese monk fell asleep while meditating and dreamed he was a butterfly. Awakening, he asking himself, "Am I a man dreaming he is a butterfly, or a butterfly dreaming he is a man?" Which is reality, which is the dream?

The Gestalt method of finishing unfinished business applies to all incomplete life situations, not only to "patients" in "therapy." To show you this, I asked Ellen, a friend who is not in any of my groups, to talk about her dreams. Ellen, a divorced teacher, and another friend, Bob, are visiting with me at my apartment on Central Park West.

Outside, eleven floors down, the 86th Street crosstown traffic shrieks and growls against the confining apartment house walls. Within, our white and green Japanese lanterns light a quiet room as Ellen lives out her dream of reality set against unreality in the dream.

JACK. I'd like for you to tell me a dream, all right?

<141>

ELLEN. I've had some interest in dreams but, trouble is, I just remember fragments, like the Fellini film, the famous Fellini Film Fragment! (*laughing*)

JACK. Mosaics from ancient Pompeii, eh? I want you to tell everything in the first person, present tense, as though you were dreaming the dream right now. Start out "I am . . . " OK?

ELLEN. I am walking in a hall that could be, could be a palace, and it's dark . . . (*pause*) The darkness is broken by lighted candles. Hooded priests are walking in a procession, couples holding these bright candles. I'm aware of the person next to me. I don't know this person, I don't remember at all, but I say to this person, "I feel like I'm in a Fellini movie." This person replies, "You *are* in a Fellini movie." Then I wake up. (*she again laughs in apparent amusement at the contradiction in the dream*) It was like a dream within a dream.

JACK. Ellen, please stand up. Actually go through the motions of your dream, remembering your experience in as much detail as possible. Experience the feeling of the stone floor under your feet, the feeling of great space in the hall, whatever.

ELLEN. (*standing hesitantly in the center of the room, shaking her head so that her long hair swirls back and forth*) I just, I just was, I was sort of . . .

JACK. (*firmly*) I *am*, I *am*, present tense.

I guide Ellen in the Now experience. Her use of the past tense and her uncertain phrasing and repeating are ways of avoiding the direct experience of the dream.

ELLEN. (*as if rehearsing*) I am, I am behind the procession. (*gaining confidence, her voice stronger*) I don't know of anyone in back of me. I'm not surrounded by people, I'm sort of following. There's a space, a feeling of . . . limited space. Mostly, it's, there's something mysterious and dark. But (*sharply*) these candles! That's it! I'm

<142>

observing more than actually participating. I'm just walking, not marching in the procession. I don't remember if the couples are in the procession. That's not clear, maybe they're just people walking. (*she walks slowly, taking a few steps*) No feeling of anything under my feet . . . it's more the, the candles . . . and not knowing where I am exactly. Just being both *in* and *not in* the procession. Just walking and then stopping. (*pause as if for instructions*)

JACK. Visualize the candle in front of you. Speak to the candle.

ELLEN. It's very hard. (*pause*)

JACK. What are you feeling?

ELLEN. I absolutely can't. I can't really relate to speaking to the candle.

JACK. Say to the candle, "I can't relate to you."

ELLEN. (*voice low, hesitating*) "I can't relate to you . . . " That doesn't feel right. (*voice surer, stronger*) I just picture a big, big tall candle sort of shining there.

JACK. (*softly*) *You* are shining there.

ELLEN. You are shining there . . . (*long pause*) Candle, there's something about you that makes me dream.

JACK. Now *be* the candle, sit over there and *be* the candle. (*Ellen obediently rises and sits in the chair opposite. She does not speak for a long moment. I prompt her*) *You* seem so dark . . .

ELLEN. (*compliant*) *You* seem so dark but . . . no . . . you don't make me feel afraid. You're a darkness that's sort of friendly . . . You're a darkness that's connected to space, a moving darkness. I see people moving through you . . . (*she pauses for several minutes, still gazing into the unseen darkness with soft eyes*)

JACK. What's happening?

ELLEN. Being the candle, I feel much more like I did in the dream. I was seeing, was looking into the darkness rather than looking at the light.

<143>

I wonder if the split, the conflict in Ellen is between light and darkness — the masculine and feminine side, Yang and Ying. I am intrigued and probe a bit further.

JACK. So your dream is looking into the darkness?

ELLEN. No, no, no, it wasn't that so much; my dream wasn't so much the candle . . . (*she falls into reverie again*)

JACK. As it was the darkness? (*I complete the sentence tentatively*)

ELLEN. (*affirming*) As it was the darkness . . . (*again gazing far away*)

Something is going on in Ellen, something not verbal. Indeed, some reverie that may or may not be directed toward my interest. Now, my concerns begin to speak up, my desire for some action, some words that can be used here in this record, plus moving Ellen to some sort of closure. Is this action to Ellen's advantage? We shall see.

JACK. Speak to the darkness.

ELLEN. I don't feel like I'm really part of the darkness. I am *behind* both the darkness and the light. I'm not dreaming that I'm *in* a Fellini movie, but it's what a Fellini movie would be like if I were watching it being made.

Ellen has split her personality into the observer (I) and the observed (darkness, light, and the Fellini movie). The integration of these selves is the goal of our dream work. The dichotomy in Ellen results in her feeling outside of her own experience. Her next action shows this.

<144>

JACK. Please put the darkness on your left side and the light on your right. You're between them and outside of them. You're the observer.

ELLEN. (*she moves to a position between the two chairs and stands expectantly for several breaths*) Hmm, that's what I experienced in my dream, a feeling of being close to the darkness and the light but not really being them . . . (*pause*) I feel like I'm outside of them both but still moving, still following them . . .

JACK. Say that to them.

ELLEN. I'm still following you. (*voice is rather expressionless as though the sentence lacks meaning for her*)

JACK. (*inquiring*) Do they reply to you? (*I'm uncertain whether this direction has life for Ellen or only represents my fantasy rather than hers*)

ELLEN. They say "You're here with us." I don't know if I feel that or I just *think* it because of the person next to me in my dream who says, "You *are* in a Fellini movie."

The darkness-light encounter hasn't revealed any gold nuggets so let's go on to the next possibility. Clearly, Ellen will have to encounter her dream shadow figure.

JACK. Now speak to that shadow person next to you in the dream.

ELLEN. Who are you? (*her face changes expression*) Oh, are you my sister?

ELLEN (*as shadow*) I, I could be your sister. That's possible because I *was* in a Fellini movie. (*Ellen looks puzzled*)

JACK. What's happening?

The inquiry, such as this, is a tool to be used sparingly. We are aiming for an experience, not an intellectual storytelling. Words

<145>

quickly convert experience into personal and meaningless bullshit. Guidance by means of words can break the flow of the pattern, the gestalten formation, yet they are nonetheless our principal tool. Therapist Jim Simkin prefers to say "What are you experiencing?" to spotlight the actual experience rather than the "thinking about" aspect.

ELLEN. My sister actually *was* a movie extra last summer in a Fellini movie in Rome. There may be a whole identification with her.

We could sure do a lot of talk about "my identification with my sister." Better get back to the encounter, quickly!

JACK. Be Ellen again (*motioning to the opposite chair*)

ELLEN. (*apparently talking to her sister*) Am I experiencing your experience? I really don't know. When you told me about it, I wanted to experience all of that excitement too. (*she sits with her eyes downward, hands crossed in her lap*)

JACK. And now?

ELLEN. I'm feeling now that maybe the shadow *wasn't* my sister; maybe it was just another part of me saying, "You don't have to wish, you *are* experiencing, now, in reality."

JACK. Say that to the shadow figure.

ELLEN. I am experiencing this.

JACK. Do you believe that?

ELLEN. I'm not totally convinced. (*Long, long pause*)

My confusion, which has been swirling around ever since Ellen began, begins to blow away like summer fog. I intuit that Ellen evades direct experience of her life by occupying the observer seat. She avoids pain by staying above what goes on in life, but not being quite "with it." Even her dream experience is insulated from reality

<146>

"like" a movie. A dream of an imitation of a replica of fantasied life. She stays away from home, from her self. The shadow, Ellen, and the sister are one. Ellen lives in confusion and takes refuge in fantasy satisfaction and make-believe reality. She uses confusion and withdrawal successfully as a defense against direct contact with her inner reality. I don't want to push much harder, for I respect her right to privacy. But I try to take the direct path now, to push for a breakthrough. If this doesn't work, I'll end the session here.

JACK. Let's go back to the darkness and the light. Find out from them if you can have the richness of a Fellini movie in real life, or if you must always pretend.

ELLEN as darkness and candles. (*silent for a while*) Yes, but you must forget about that person next to you, think only of the lightness and the darkness and the candles and the people. Then you can really enjoy and be yourself without even thinking, "Is this a Fellini movie or not?"

I don't understand — forget the shadow self? Concentrate on the external world? "Put your awareness into reality instead of yourself" may be the meaning.

JACK. (*laughing*) Maybe I've guessed it now. Put the shadow next to you and say, "I am experiencing directly. I don't need you. I have myself."

ELLEN. (*talking to chair, without expression*) I am experiencing directly. I don't need you. I have myself.

JACK. Say that again.

ELLEN. (*more firmly*) I am experiencing directly. I don't need you. I have myself.

<147>

That's better; to base Ellen's statement in Now experience, we go to the body language in order to begin awareness of her rigid isolation from direct contact with herself, as well as her social world.

JACK. How does the way you're standing feel to you?

ELLEN. I feel very stiff.

Good, a direct uncomplicated perception! Let's follow up, by jumping over to the opposite case, like rocking a car back and forth to get it out of a muddy spot.

JACK. That's right. You *are* stiff. OK, now try the opposite: "I *do* need you. I'm not myself." (*laughs*)

ELLEN. I just, I just had a really wild idea ... (*she also laughs and waves her hands*)

JACK. Do that again! (*Ellen repeats with a larger gesture*) Whe-shuooo!

ELLEN. A really wild idea of running off, into the space and joining the procession! Like this! (*hands in front as though carrying a candle, she begins walking with slow steps*) I was really getting, getting more and more outside of that procession (*laughs*) and then all of a sudden I get into it! How I basically dig being part of the procession, part of the situation! (*circles around the room in a graceful dance*)

JACK. You really get right into the real experience. Beautiful!

Let's give Ellen some "wins." Everybody needs "wins." This is a breakthrough, just when I had given up. And very likely, *because* I gave up and got my expectations of Ellen out of the way.

JACK. What's happening now?

<150>

<148>

ELLEN. I just talked to the shadow and she said, "You *are* in a Fellini movie — you are in it all the time," and just like that I let go.

JACK. Well! Do you want to continue a bit to find out what "she" means by "being in a Fellini movie"?

The question here is whether to quit as a winner, with this breakthrough to direct experience of life or to shoot for double or nothing.

JACK. Ask the shadow.

ELLEN. What does being in a Fellini movie mean (*speaking to empty chair opposite her*)?

ELLEN as shadow. (*her voice is more resonant, older*) It means you *are* in it all the time. The life you live every day is like a Fellini movie.

ELLEN. Why do you think it's like a *Fellini* movie, why *him* of all people?

ELLEN as shadow. Because of the atmosphere, the mystery, the strangeness and strange kind of people, the excitement.

ELLEN. My dream reminds me of *La Dolce Vita* or some movie like that. It seems *like* I'm sitting and observing, *like* I'm just remembering it. But I'm not really in it.

ELLEN as shadow. But you *are* in it, in your life. You're standing right here, right now and you're in the procession. You're moving with it. It is it, it is all of us. (*pause — Ellen seems puzzled*)

JACK. Replace the "it" with "I."

Recall that replacing the impersonal "it" with the personal "I" brings home the personal significance. "It" is outside of me. "I" is inside.

<149>

ELLEN. (*uncertain*) *I* am it?

JACK. It?

ELLEN. (*laughs*) I *am* I ... oh! (*understanding and delight on her face*) I am *I*, *I* am in the procession and *I* am moving with *me*. I am *me*.

JACK. Say that again.

ELLEN. (*more definitely*) *I am me!*

COMMENTS

Yes, indeed, I am me and Ellen has joined the procession of life. She has acknowledged and experienced her shadow as self. She doesn't have to sit in the audience and watch life being performed onstage. She is on stage, in the eternal game we call life. This is the center, the core. Ellen affirms Ellen. No if, and, or but. *I am me*. I can't be any more and I won't be any less. I AM ME. Try that little phrase yourself. I am me. Listen to your voice. Any hesitation? Any fading? Any question marks? Any undue loudness or softness? Any phoniness? Say it to a couple of friends. What do they hear? Compose a chant, a mantrum. Put the mantrum in your heart; whistle it on the subway. Keep on until you find yourself answering, "Yes, that's right — *I am me!*"

POSTDREAM DISCUSSION WITH ELLEN AND BOB

BOB. You said Ellen had reached her impasse, her third level?

ELLEN. Yes, I really did.

BOB. Did you get out of it?

ELLEN. I think, I *feel* I did.

<150>

JACK. She got through it. (*to Ellen*) You moved out of your observer-play pretend attitude when you started to dance. Your body took over, and your body never lies, never deceives. Not all the way out of your impasse, but a long way out of your detachment, your unreality of being an observer-outsider to life. You joined the procession instead of sitting on the sidelines.

ELLEN. Yes! Yes!

JACK. You joined the unity, the flow of life that allows no room for bystanders, observers. Your inner self, your shadow, knew, knows the real trip. In your fear of being hurt by actual experience, the external "you" labeled the dream, the real-life experience "just a dream imitation of a Fellini movie."

BOB. What is the real trip?

JACK. The real trip is reality. What is. No more, no less. A lot of reality isn't pleasant, isn't what I planned on, but I can at least look at it straight instead of fooling myself. In the Arica training we call that reality "being in the pattern." Ellen's dream calls it "being in the procession." Both are beautiful. Both know that every event, every person, every thing fits together in the supreme gestalt, the unity of oneness that is perfect. In reality there is simply being, total being. There are no splits, no conflicts, no duality, no here-there, now-then, mine-yours, good-bad. Only in the mind is the conflict of duality. (*to Ellen*) Your original split was the observer and the observed. But you found out for yourself that your personal split was healed when you got out of dualism, out of being the observer of life, into the flow, into your procession. That clearness and happiness is what we call "satori."

ELLEN. Just being in that space is so beautiful. I want to dance again. (*pause*) You know, when you first asked me to speak to the light, I couldn't relate to it. I felt very uptight — the lights were so scattered, so far away really, so intermingled with the darkness. I could only picture this huge candle which suddenly came up in front

<151>

of my face, like a zoom shot of a camera. I couldn't relate to it on a real basis.

JACK. You could relate to the darkness more? Ah so, the ying and the yang. You related to the Mother and not to the Father which is light. The Mother, the darkness you described as mysterious and friendly is the Earth Mother, the night chaos, the primal Mother. That darkness in the womb out of which we come by reason of the stimulus of the energy of the Father — that stimulus felt as energy, as light, by the ovum.

ELLEN. (*excited*) Of course, of course! The big big candle is like the phallic symbol. I, I actually thought of that but (*shyly*), I didn't say anything. (*blushing*) It didn't fit! (*loud laughter from all of us*)

BOB. Can you explain "ying" and "yang"?

JACK. Chinese terms for the duality, the polarity, the opposing, interlinked forces of the universe. Yang is the thrusting, hard, active masculine. Ying is the soft, attractive, feminine, the receptive. We Westerners forget that the ying must be, and *is,* equally strong as the yang, in order for the universe to be balanced. Femininity is just as strong as masculinity.

<152>

13

My Mother, the Maniac Behind the Wheel

Sylvia is the highly educated product of a wealthy Eastern family. She has done graduate work at an Ivy League college and is within nodding distance of her Ph.D. Now she is at the graduate school of direct life experience, working as a member of the Esalen staff.

She has chosen to sit in on my workshop this morning. I am flattered; Esalen staff members have their pick of the world's best know-yourself techniques, and Sylvia's choosing my workshop is an indication I must be doing something right.

A lovely, warm, wholesome-looking woman, Sylvia has a slight twist to the right side of her lip, where a scar runs from near the upper canine tooth up along her nose. Her charming smile has a slight extra upward tilt from this scar. Having asked to work, she sits in the hot seat and plunges into her dream.

SYLVIA. I'm in the car with mother again, and she's driving. It's a car we shared when I was in high school. She's driving and I'm in the passenger seat. I can see her at the wheel ... and she's just intense.

<153>

Her eyes are bugged the way my eyes get bugged. Like this. (*Sylvia leans forward, both hands on an imaginary steering wheel, face tense, eyes widely opened and fixed straight ahead*) She's just fierce. It's like her tense energy is the motor that's driving the car. And I can see her. Then I go outside and I look in the car. It's dark all around and I can barely see myself. I'm like a hovering presence. She's carting me off, back to Barnes College ... that's where I went to college. I hated it.

JACK. "I hate it" — present tense. "I hate it."

SYLVIA. I hate it. I hate Barnes. I don't want to go back there. I never wanted to go there to begin with. You maneuvered me. You manipulated me into going there. And it was the worst place in the world for ...

JACK. "It is ... "

SYLVIA. It *is* the worst place in the world for me. I hate it. it's a small dink-shit institution. And *you* had to have me go there. Because it's your ego that's riding on it. And I had to go there and do well so you could impress all your alumni friends. (*pause*)

JACK. Is that the end of your dream?

SYLVIA. Yeah. Yeah, that was the end of the dream.

Well, there's certainly not much problem in deciding which way to go. Mama is certainly the cheese sandwich in *this* grill.

JACK. Now, be your mother in the dream.

SYLVIA. (*she makes a sour face, then obediently settles herself in the clumsy lawn chair with a deep breath. Her voice changes to a rheumy monopausal rasp*) I'm *all* correct ... there's nothing ... Well, I *know* what's best for you. You just don't *know*. I know what's absolutely *best*. Whatever you do, I'm going to take you where you belong. 'Cause I *know*. And I'm just going to screw up all my energy and take you there whether you *want* to go or not. And I don't give a *shit* about

<154>

what you think. Or *what* you want to do or *who* you are. You're just here to fulfill *my* expectations. And man, you'd better *do* it. And I'm just gonna . . . I don't care if you become a hovering presence like a vague cloud. Just as long as you're in my car *I'm* driving.

JACK. What do you feel?

SYLVIA. I feel tightness. I feel clenched. I feel constipated. She's *been* constipated all her life.

JACK. Let your mother speak.

SYLVIA as mother. I've been constipated all my life. One of my main problems. (*oddly, there's a tone of pride in her voice*) Yeah, I hold on.

SYLVIA. A real tight-ass.

SYLVIA as mother. I don't let people know that, though. I come across as being very gentle and sweet and innocent and wouldn't hurt a fly. (*simpering*) I'm just sweet little Lucy.

JACK. All right. Be your mother on the toilet.

SYLVIA as mother. (*there are cheers from the audience as she bends forward, bears down, and emits loud grunts and groans. Her face becomes flushed*) Well, it sure fills me full of energy.

JACK. But nothing's coming out. OK, be your mother's asshole.

Being this scatological is a matter of judgment as to the level of inhibition in Sylvia. With some people I wouldn't feel comfortable in giving these directions. They couldn't handle the situation. I intuit that Sylvia is past a great deal of her shame about excretion. She can get down to fundamentals.

SYLVIA. (*as herself*) I'm also flashing that holding in, that feeling of constipation is this right side. That's just what this right side does. It pulls in like this. (*she squeezes right arm against her side, while the lip scar becomes more evident*)

<155>

JACK. That's right. So play your mother's asshole.

SYLVIA as asshole. Well, I'm *tight*. And, I'm *small*. And I'm not going to let anything out. I'm going to keep all my goodies for myself. And I'm not going to let anyone know there's stuff in there. 'Cause they might want it. And I'm not going to let it out. I'm going to keep closed off. You just feed all good stuff into me. And I'll just keep it in. And also ... what comes out might not be pleasant. And that also frightens me. I might not like what comes out. I might not like to see ... my shit.

SYLVIA as mother. I don't *want* to see my shit. I want to be perfect. I don't ... I don't ... (*voice drops*) I don't pee and shit like other people. I'm perfect, and I don't have any of that stuff.

Sylvia, as Sylvia, is open and unashamed of her excretions. But within her personality is that of her mother, who is entirely the opposite. The mother aspect demands perfection, which is being entirely unnatural: "I don't pee and shit like other people." All the components for a serious personality conflict are present. Let's bring the conflict out into the open.

JACK. Now be Sylvia. Talk to your mother's asshole.

SYLVIA. You're full of shit! (*a little defensive, as though afraid of what she has said to her mother*) Well, that's the truth! By holding that stuff in you're making yourself tight and uncomfortable. You go through awful stuff. You know ... you drink mineral water and Phillip's Milk of Magnesia and stuff like that. And you're not going to be happy until you just open up and let the process flow. You're blocking process. And by holding on, you're paralyzing ... paralyzing ... fixating ... you're? ... (*Sylvia has noticed that her right hand is holding tightly to the left hand, so tightly that the knuckles are white*)

JACK. You feel that (*indicating the clenched hand*)?

<156>

SYLVIA. Yes, the right hand . . . this right hand is just holding onto the left. The left is . . . the left is flowing . . . the left wants to move.

Our old friend, the right-left split, is here in all its glory. The right hand is mother and control; the left is self and freedom. Sylvia has manifested her conflict with mother as an internal conflict between these two aspects of herself. Let's transfer Sylvia's awareness from the me-mother split to the left-right split.

JACK. Let your left hand say, "I want to flow."

SYLVIA as left hand. I want to flow. I want to move. I want to be easy. I want things to pass through me and out of me. I don't want . . . I don't want to be grasped at by you, right hand. I don't want to be possessed by you or held by you. I want to be open and easy and gentle. (*she looks down at her hands as a child does, noticing, as though for the first time, their unique identity*)

JACK. What does the right hand say?

SYLVIA as right hand. Right hand says, left hand, you just don't know what's good for you. I know what's good. And I can pull and push and arrange the world. And control and manipulate. And I can protect you from getting hurt. I can . . . I can make things safe for you. (*long pause*) I'll make your world a whole lot smaller too. I'll keep you from being fully yourself. I'll hit on you and I'll scare you. And then you'll be closed-off like me. (*long pause*) The right hand says now all I really want is love. And I want care. I don't know how to ask for it so I hit. (*pause*)

SYLVIA. The left hand is lighter than my right hand. The right hand is heavy.

JACK. Let the right hand stay heavy.

SYLVIA as right hand. I'm heavy. I'm heavy-handed. I'm heavy-handed. And you, left hand, are lighter. You're a floating hand. And

<157>

I'm heavy. And I'd like to be light. Lighter. Now my hands seem to be equalling out a bit. And I'm checking out my eyes to see if it's happening there.

JACK. Check out the sides of your face. Right side, then left side.

SYLVIA. Well, the right side is still . . .

JACK. Let the right side speak. "I'm still . . . "

SYLVIA as right side. I'm still a little tense. I'm still a little tense. And I'm still tighter than you, left side. And . . . I've given you, left side, some of my energy. I can feel you more now. It doesn't . . . I'm aware of it right here. The holding is right here. And this side . . . I can feel it out of there. (*she indicates with her right hand a position about four inches from the right side of her face*)

JACK. Let's try an experiment. Now let's turn and look at each other. Now look in my eyes . . . look in my left eye, OK? Now become aware of your face. (*we are directly facing one another, each looking into the other's left eye*)

SYLVIA. My right side seems squished up. Like this. (*she contracts her right facial muscles into a grimace*)

JACK. Now, as we look at each other's eyes, consciously become aware of the tensions in your face and let go of them and relax.

Over a period of four or five minutes first her forehead loses deep furrows, then the cheeks and chin become soft. Finally the slight snarling tension of the nostrils goes, leaving only the scar on the right upper lip.

JACK. Stay with the awareness of your face. And, as you find a tense area in your face, let your awareness go there. And just iron it out. (*pause*) Now close your eyes and hold that relaxation. (*pause*) Be aware of your face muscles. Search out and let go. At this point concentrate around the eyes. Be aware of the tension in your left eyelid. Now put your awareness into the area where you have scars,

<158>

like your right nostril. Put your awareness where you have scars. (*pause*) Imagine that you are breathing through the right side of your face. As you breathe, air is going in and out of the right side of your face. (*pause*) How does your face feel?

SYLVIA. I feel . . . (*inaudible mumble*) and I still have a skull fracture back here. And my facial scars are . . . (*inaudible) the skull fracture.*

JACK. Oh, you have a basal skull fracture? (*pause, still looking into her eyes*) Let your awareness go back into there, into the fracture. Relax your face first. (*after several minutes I reach my hands out and put my right hand behind Sylvia's head while I massage her facial scar with my left hand. Sylvia begins to breathe heavily and to move her head under my hand, as though to avoid the pressure, yet not breaking away*) That's it, make some noise.

SYLVIA. (*first loud pants, then suddenly screams in terror over and over again, sobbing loudly*)

JACK. Say *"No!"*

SYLVIA. *No! No! No! No!* (*sobbing*)

JACK. Keep on saying, *No! Mother!"*

SYLVIA. Mother . . . mother, *No! No! Mother! No!* (*screams*) NO NO NO NO NO . . . no!

JACK. Like this. (*I hit my fist on the table*)

SYLVIA. (*hitting table with each "No!"*) No! No! I won't let you break me. I won't let you break me! *I won't let you break me! No!* (*slam, slam, slam, slam*) *No! You . . . No!* (*pause*)

JACK. Do you feel like going on, or do you want to stop here?

SYLVIA. (*long pause*) I'd like to go on, I'd like to finish her.

JACK. I'm going to massage the base of your skull where you had the fracture; what was it, a car accident?

<159>

SYLVIA. Yes, we were arguing and she didn't see a car coming from the left. I was thrown out of the car.

JACK. OK, I'll stop any time you say to stop. (*I brace her head with my right hand. With my left I rub lightly at first below and behind Sylvia's right ear. When I feel her stiffen, I apply increasing pressure. She begins moaning*)

SYLVIA. That hurts . . . it's so sore.

JACK. Let yourself go back to the accident, feel the accident.

SYLVIA. Damn you, *damn you damn you*! You saw that car, you saw it! You will get your way if you have to kill me! (*pause; heavy breathing*) *Stop! Don't!* You're hurting me! (*she sobs loudly. I hand her a tissue*) I can't do any more. (*long pause*)

JACK. How does your face feel now?

SYLVIA. That's funny, now I feel the right side more clearly. There's still a dead spot here (*touching her right cheek near the nostril*), but the right and left sides feel almost the same.

JACK. Check out your entire self, check out the whole right and left.

SYLVIA. Huh — right arm is still a bit stiffer, left feels nearly as strong. I'm more in balance, I'm almost entirely in balance.

JACK. Let's stop here, OK?

SYLVIA. Yes, I'd like to. Thank you, Jack.

JACK. *De nada*. Thank you.

COMMENTARY ON SYLVIA'S DREAMWORK

Even with a young woman such as Sylvia, bright, open-minded, adventurous, and exposed to all sorts of awareness therapies, we still find the conflict, the *paralyzing* conflict between her past experience (in the form of memory) and her present reality. We see in Sylvia a very strong right-left split, an adult-youth split, and of course the

<160>

usual social adjustment-spontaneity split. These conflicts cause the tension that was so evident in her face.

All I have been able to do is help Sylvia contact her conflict level, her uncompleted gestalt. She then worked her way through her fear, that restricting tension causing fear, and released her own life energy. The result was a dramatic change in her facial muscles — a softening, a relaxing.

Sylvia's dream states what happens to many young people at different levels of society. Parents, school, society, say (quoting Sylvia's mother), "I don't give a shit about what you think. Or what you want to do or who you are. You're just here to fulfill my expectations. And man, you'd better do it . . . I don't care if you become a vague, hovering presence like a cloud. As long as you're in my car, I'm driving." And, unfortunately, some young people *do* become "vague clouds." They never do find their own real identities but go through life trying on one "social" role after another. Often by denying young people the responsible freedom to try out their own new lifestyles we force them to rebel completely. It's too bad, for in the complete rebellion of youth much of the *valid* wisdom of the past is lost.

What I have done by massaging Sylvia's scalp and facial muscles is physically pinpoint the focus of her conflict, the memory (remembered and suppressed) of her mother's domination. By concentrating, becoming more aware, living through, actually *re*living through the pain and fear of that memory, Sylvia has unified and freed her energy. She will exist as a more harmonious, more productive human being now.

Those of us who fail to recognize that there is no difference between the seemingly different levels of existence — physical reality, inside-the-self intrapsychic reality, interpersonal reality, social reality, and so on — are doomed to go through life in constant and wasteful conflict with ourselves and with the world. Reality is a unity with different views or angles glimpsed through different peepholes of the perceptual mind.

<161>

The manner in which many of us go through life reminds me of a great excavation site where a great construction project has been scheduled to begin. But, alas, the project boss, the single person who is able to coordinate it all and make it work, is missing. So the job is left to the sidewalk superintendents. Each of them stands around the building excavation behind those boards perforated with sidewalk peepholes. Each successive peephole gives a different, greatly limited view of the grand proceeding. A pile driver here, a giant ball and crane over there, a couple of dump trucks at another spot. What happens is that each of these loudmouth sidewalk superintendents, stationed at their own personal peephole, announces with great certainty that his is the only *true* peephole, and *his* is the only *reliable* account of whatever processes are going on inside the walls. Attracted by the noise, a crowd gathers around each superintendent to agree, disagree, or simply gawk. Observations are made, theories elaborated, orthodoxies and heresies promulgated, interpeephole commissions appointed. Experts give *expert* opinions on variations in observable phenomena. Peephole University has been created, endowed, and made eternal. Meanwhile, the excavation continues.

<162>

14

Earth, Air, and Water: Cyndy's Two Dreams

Most of the dreams in this book are unfinished business, rooted in neurotic conflicts. They are unfinished life patterns pushing to be completed. For some of us who have lived through and worked out enough of our problems, the dream mechanism can go beyond neurosis into direct experience of a variety of life vibrating all around us. Once our eyes and ears and mind and body are cleansed of the debris we call "neurosis," we can and do tune in on the rest of the universe. (For a longer discussion of this fact, I refer you to my friend John Lilly's autobiography, *Center of the Cyclone*)

Cyndy is a bright, cheerful woman who has paid her dues by a great deal of personal exploration. We are friends of long standing; both of us teach at the San Francisco Gestalt Institute; and we enjoy doing workshops together. She offers the following dream experience, which shows the excitement and rewards of going beyond conventional therapy. This dream experience enlarges her, gives her direct links to the bigger reality around her and within her.

<163>

Our work takes place at the Gestalt Institute in a bright room overlooking a small park from which sounds of children playing are heard.

CYNDY. Are you going to want to Gestalt me with this too?

JACK. What I'd like to do is to work on it with you.

CYNDY. Great! Well, I'm going to tell you the background because that's as important as the dreams. And this is all occurring two or three years ago and is one of the most powerful experiences of my life.

JACK. You seem very happy about it.

CYNDY. Oh, *yes*! (*laughs*) You may have been there, Jack. It was at Bridge Mountain, I think the first weekend we had a trainee workshop.

JACK. Don't think so ... no, I don't remember being there.

Actually, I *was* there. The Bridge Mountain Foundation of Ben Lomond, California, is a warm, rustic lodge high in the coastal redwood forest. In the loose camaraderie of the growth centers, the Gestalt Institute uses the facilities at Bridge Mountain for its own informal training programs.

CYNDY. It was in the evening, and I brought my costumes down. It was the first time we had costumes. Saturday night, and I remember Ricky making up my eyes. The costume I put on was a black Afro wig. My eyes were made up to look Egyptian, and then I had on just a Madras long dress. As the evening wore on, people were playing and dancing until the music went off. There were three or four people playing the drums. I was standing, I'll tell it in the present tense, I'm standing beside Jerry Rothsteen (*of the Gestalt Institute of Canada*) and some other people, and I have on my outfit. Usually in this kind of situation I'm out there dancing but something in me didn't feel like

<164>

dancing. (*she gets up and moves to center of room*) I'm standing on the side watching everyone else dance. I have my foot like this (*left foot extended*). I'm starting to tap, and pretty soon I'm chanting. I'm making sounds I've never heard before. Pretty soon I lose total self-consciousness of everyone there, although I'm very aware of their presence. I chant and chant and chant, making sounds I've never heard in myself before. My sense was of being, not in this life, but a previous life. Of having been an old, middle-aged woman at a tribal dance. The power of that experience was profound (*voice hushed*), and it was like I was there, but I *wasn't* there. I have a vision of myself chanting that night ... I went to sleep scared and I woke up scared. I was running around asking, "What happened to me? What did I look like?" all that day. That day was Sunday. Then I came back (home). The next two nights I have *very* powerful dreams. And those followed this incident. Do you want me to go into the first dream?

JACK. Yes.

CYNDY. OK. Ah, the first night I go to sleep. I don't remember whether my body was tight or not. I think I was still anxious about what had happened. I didn't know what to *do* with the experience.

JACK. I *don't* know, present tense.

CYNDY. I don't know what to do. Now I'm asleep. I'm ah ... I'm going. I don't see how my body looks, all I know I'm in my body, and I'm going down through the earth. I feel like, like I'm falling and I'm aware of thinking I'm dying, and I'm sinking through the layers of the earth and the earth is brown, red brown, and almost looking like a geography map of the slices of the earth. And I go through, feeling some *very* pleasurable feelings, even though I am saying to myself, "I'm dying." I get down to a certain place, I'm not sure where, and I move off to the left, and all of a sudden I'm in the ocean. I start swimming with the fish, and I feel absolutely fantastic. Everything is very colorful ... lots of blues and sparkly whites like when the sun hits the water. The fish are kind of moving with me. We're gliding along together.

<165>

JACK. You're a fish?

CYNDY. I'm Cyndy and I'm a fish. I can't differentiate. I breathe in there, and I'm alive and I feel wonderful and there are lots of very gentle fish moving with me. (*voice is smooth and purling like gentle ocean waves*) And we got, everything is brilliant, ah, ah, this is a feeling I've never had before, some pleasure feeling I don't recall having had before. Ah . . .

JACK. *Never?*

CYNDY. Huh-uh.

JACK. Let yourself experience that pleasure now.

CYNDY. I'm feeling it right now. And here (*indicating lower abdomen*) and at the base of my spine, my buttocks, and what else . . . (*sighs softly*)

JACK. Put your awareness down there.

CYNDY. I'm also aware of my eyes fluttering and my arms tingling . . . When I put my attention back here, I feel like something's opened . . . (*indicates lower spine*)

Sounds very much like Cyndy is experiencing the opening of the sacral or Muladahara chakra, one of the eight psychophysiological centers of combined automatic nervous system and endocrine gland function.

JACK. Now let your breathing go down into your pelvis.

CYNDY. I want to sit out here . . . yeah. (*moves into center of room*)

JACK. Let yourself be a *fish*, a fish swimming along, you have a tail and you're moving from that point in the base of your spine, that's the point you move from, you have a tail . . . (*Cyndy lies on her belly, extends arms and legs in swimming movement*) You're moving from that point in the base of your spine. That's the point you move from

<166>

... (*she continues to swim*) And let yourself feel how this is. This *is* the level of energy for your fish level.

CYNDY. I feel like I have a motor back there.

I begin to realize that swimming is the essence of fishness. Seemingly, a fish's life center is the swimming center. All else is secondary.

JACK. You *do* have a motor back there, yeah.

In order to help develop Cyndy's chakra awareness, I start to chant the vibratory mode appropriate to that particular chakra. This is a traditional Hindu technique.

CYNDY. I recognize that. One of your chakras, isn't it?

JACK. What are you experiencing now?

CYNDY. I'm going back and forth from just feeling the sound to mind-fucking about whether I should still be moving or not ...

JACK. Just feel the sound, feel how your center is down there, your mover. (*Cyndy breathes slowly*)

CYNDY. I can feel that center more as I move it. And it's a very unusual experience to feel a motor there. I mean I can *feel* how that can propel me through the water. I feel very ripply like water ... I just, I sense all the other fish around me all ripply with me ... (*delighted chuckle*) and somehow at my head all is reaction to my motor ... It starts there and all the rest of me moves as a result of that ripple ... ripple (*sound of exhalation of air*) ... I feel like reaching out ...

JACK. Now let yourself be aware of all the other fishes ... Enter into the group mind of the whole school of fishes. Let your awareness expand until you are in touch with the whole group mind of this whole group of fishes ... Let yourself feel how the group mind

<167>

controls the school's formation. Each component fish in your mind moves as one . . .

CYNDY. (*awe in voice*) Huh! Oh wow!j I feel them coming off the side of my body . . . 'cause they, you know, they are out there . . . I feel they're here and here on down my legs and I just felt them here (*indicating both sides of torso*) which is an area where someone was working on me once. I just cried, it was incredibly beautiful. The fish touch me, I'm experiencing their energy touching me. And that somehow there's nobody in control . . . it's like we all, we all *know* . . .

JACK. We all know . . . ?

CYNDY. Together . . .

JACK. Yes, that's right. That's the energy of the motor you feel. That's life energy . . . Feel that energy . . . that energy and intelligence . . . together.

CYNDY. God, it feels really beautiful, all moving together . . . hum, I feel very . . . the word doesn't sound right on one level . . . taken care of. I feel *surrounded*, warm, touching energy . . . I feel bathed all the way around . . . I'm aware now of my being the biggest fish although I'm still Cyndy. The fishes around me are maybe that big (*holds hands about sixteen inches apart*) but there are lots of them. Like a battleship with a lot of little tug boats around it.

JACK. Big Fish Cyndy . . .

CYNDY. (*voice lightens and is almost childish*) And I feel younger than them. Like they know this trip better than me and they're kind of taking care of me and showing me how beautiful . . .

JACK. Well, speak to them.

CYNDY. You're really taking care of me. Without saying anything you are showing me how to move in this kind of atmosphere. How to ripple and how to feel your presence up and down my sides . . . Usually I don't pay attention to my sides. But that's where I feel you.

<168>

And I feel something different on my belly and back. My belly feels very warm, and I don't feel you under me. And I don't feel you on top of me and that's all right . . . Somehow I know you're not going to leave me . . . I trust you . . . (*contented sigh*)

Is it possible that fish have pressure receptors only along their sides? That these receptors sense the "ripples" from adjacent fish and thus are the way in which schools of fish swim in that amazingly coordinated fashion? Cyndy seems to be experiencing that same kind of "rippling" on her sides only.

Knowing Cyndy as well as I do, I decide to take the chance of plunging her into a deeper experience — an awareness of two perceptions at once. Most people in our society are so rigidly trained as to focus on one perception at a time. This limitation is considered "normal." Yet there have been reports of those who have been sufficiently developed to have been aware of twelve perceptions simultaneously. I have enough confidence in Cyndy's development to believe she can absorb a dual or multiple perception.

JACK. Let yourself remain one with the fish . . . and let yourself get in touch with the African woman at the same time.

CYNDY. (*long pause*) It's hard . . . I go back and forth . . .

JACK. All right, get in touch with the African woman first then . . .

CYNDY. And what . . . I'm into, and I'm not sure whether I'm thinking this or experiencing it, but a sense of trying to get in touch with the chanting *inside*, whereas I'm feeling the fishes *outside* of me. The chanting was something that was opening up something *inside* . . . You understanding what I'm trying to say?

JACK. Uh-huh.

CYNDY So I'm inside my body and feeling it kind of opening . . . although I'm still feeling the fishes around me . . .

<169>

JACK. Stay with the fishes, don't lose the fishes . . .

CYNDY. They're still there.

JACK. See if you can move also to the level of the African woman, and the Earth . . . Get in touch with the great Mother.

CYNDY. I just feel this *huge* open space in the inside of my body. And my vagina's not a vagina, it's just like a *huge*, opening, and it goes into the earth . . . and it's a beautiful feeling. (*softly*)

JACK. *I'm* a beautiful feeling.

CYNDY. I'm a beautiful feeling . . . I'm now tripping out on being an earth sign with a lot of water in my horoscope.

JACK. Stay with it, it's all right.

CYNDY. I'm really *feeling* that . . . wow!

JACK. Yeah, feel it, feel your sigh.

CYNDY. Whooo! (*soft sigh*)

Whatever the "truth" of astrology — and I truly have no personal opinion other than that science is one thing and psychic reality another — there *is* a psychic reality to these great and eternal concepts. That psychic reality is what Cyndy is experiencing now. I believe that in Jungian terms, she is contacting certain archetypes, great mental forces, which lie latent in all of us, and which are capable of being stirred into consciousness by the appropriate internal or external stimulus.

JACK. Put that energy you feel into the earth. Down through your vagina into the earth and feel how as you do that, how the energy enters into you, so you are transmitting the energy into Mother Earth.

CYNDY. I'm sending it *down?*

<170>

JACK. You're sending it down; it's passing through you into the earth . . .

CYNDY. I feel shaped like that (*sketches inverted triangle in air*) a reverse triangle or a funnel . . . Almost like I can't, I'm not as wide as I feel . . . I'm seeing blue lights going down . . . (*long pause; soft sigh*) Oh, now it's become a river . . .

JACK. *I've* become a river . . .

CYNDY. I've become a river . . . I just go and I go and I go and I'm experiencing that the earth is just *endless* and my river is . . . I'm experiencing me as the river . . . and my river is just going *down* … my river is quieting down somewhat and as the fish I feel quieted down, somewhat quieted down, and not moving so fast through the water . . . hummm, hummm I'm seeing a lot of aqua color. Before, I was seeing purple. I'm seeing aqua . . . I'm the African woman again, and I'm feeling very strong and quiet and — ah — like I would be comfortable sitting like this for a long time (*legs crossed on floor*) … I feel a lot of energy in my back here and here (*lower belly and back*). I don't want to move.

JACK. Don't, don't. This is your life energy, your life force energy...

CYNDY. I feel *really rooted* now, and uh . . . (*long pause*) . . . I'm feeling a little scared letting my eyes do this.

JACK. Do you want to go any further?

CYNDY I've done all I want to do . . .

JACK. Yeah. You *are* in touch with your energies of life, which are separate from the energies of the heart or of the mind . . . really different, though basically one . . .

CYNDY. That was really interesting, feeling both the woman and the fish.

JACK. Well, you're both an earth and water sign . . . how do you feel now?

<171>

CYNDY. Oh, I feel *good* . . . I remember once when I saw a picture in some big photograph book, and it was the only picture that attracted my attention. It was of an African woman underneath a tree in a kind of meadow. I can't remember how the woman was standing but it was not that far from how I expressed myself that night at the party. That had happened a year or so before that night at Bridge Mountain . . .

JACK. What does this experience mean to you?

CYNDY. This one, or the whole thing?

CYNDY. The whole thing.

CYNDY. I'm not sure, other than experiencing that kind of depth again, like how I felt the woman and the chanting . . . I'm not scared of that now, the dream, and when I was chanting . . . and what I make of that is like going back to something that has been blocked or that I haven't allowed myself to experience more often. It's like opening up a cavern, um, sort of feels like a *vessel* . . . (*pause*) Do you want to hear the other one? The next night?

JACK. Yes. What happened the next night?

CYNDY. If you get into the horoscope trip, the next night is, uh, the air signs . . . I don't know if I have any air signs in my chart, not very heavily . . . well, OK. I'm in a space ship . . . I drowned last night; now I'm in a space ship! (*laughs*) And I'm . . . I'm reminded in the space ship of being in the movie *2001*, although my space ship is not that large . . . And the air and sky around me is very blue, brilliant blue again. I'm very colorful. And I'm, I'm shooting out, everything is very sharply defined, unlike the water and the earth. The quality of the feeling is different and I can't describe it. Not like being in the water, uh, I feel slightly cool on the edge of my skin. I feel peaceful, I don't feel exhilarated; I feel peaceful. That's not the right word . . . yes, it's up here (*indicates the chest*) some feeling in my chest area as I go up. (*her voice has changed; it's louder, clearer, lighter than before*)

<172>

JACK. Could it be described as "my heart is uplifted"?

CYNDY. (*doubtfully*) Yeah, yeah, I feel as though I'm moving from here (*again indicating center of chest*). And going up. That's very interesting, I hadn't gotten into that. Even though my head is going first, I don't feel like it's my head . . .

JACK. Your center this time is in your chest . . .

CYNDY. So, I keep going up and up, and the next thing I'm aware of, I'm on another planet. And I'm in a warehouse, a natural wood building like an old warehouse or an old barn that has booths in it that are open. So you walk down and all you see are open booths. And as I'm walking down all I see are what's on tables in the booths, and feet of many people. I don't see the people. And I go into one booth, and there's a beautiful red patchwork velvet dress that I just love. And I want it. And I know it's not my dress. I don't know how I know, I just know it's not my dress. So I keep going down and don't see any people, I just see lots of feet. And I go to see a few more dresses, lots of bright velvets and patchwork prints, and finally I come to the last booth. There is a royal rich blue dress with beads, all kinds of beautiful colored beads on the bodice, and I know that's my dress ... and I wake up. After the dream I went to the store and made the dress and spent three days on the beads, just doing a trip on the while thing. I changed the dress style and made it. And that's the dream. Again very brilliant. The colors in the first dream were more muted, very colorful though less brilliant.

JACK. OK, would you put the dress there and speak to the dress?

CYNDY. I almost brought it today to show you. I should have.

JACK. I wish you had. Would you describe the dress, please.

CYNDY. I took a few yards of blue velveteen and cut a hole in it, so when you put it over your head and stand up and put your arms out, it goes *out* to the side. I put a hood on it and the tassels on the hood are strung beads. Then I have three layers of beads on the front.

<173>

JACK. Put the dream dress there in front of you.

CYNDY. You are very bright. You're very rich, ah ... you're soft and you, when the light hits you different ways you change. I'm thinking of the water again, sometimes parts of you look silver. Your beads are all bright reds and yellows and lime green and white. I'm aware of my hand shaking ... you're soft, very soft ... you feel good ... I feel like there's something, I don't know how to describe it, about your conformity ... and when I put you on, oh wow! I feel very, very ... soft ... and very loose. And you flow and you look wonderful and I move around and go in all these different directions wherever the energy ... you feel cozy and warm ... and I'm aware now, Jack, that my head feels buzzy and my arms, I feel really full right now.

JACK. What do you feel in your chest?

CYNDY. I feel full there ... and now I'm feeling a slight tightness and a slight feeling of yearning coming through, like a reaching from here (*indicating chest*). Before, it was more continuing ... I'm aware of blocking ...

JACK. Have you ever felt anything as soft as this dress before?

CYNDY. (*softly*) No ... Now my chest is feeling very warm on the left side ...

JACK. What color is the warmth, does it have a color?

CYNDY. I'm seeing yellow ... a mild burning that's pleasurable.

JACK. Visualize that warmth as the sun, the full golden warm sun ...

CYNDY. I feel *so* warm ... I don't feel it down in my belly. Just in my chest, and more on the left than on the right ...

JACK. Now see if you can feel the warmth in your chest and the feeling you had in your previous dream, at the same time.

<174>

CYNDY. I just brought back the fishes! They are on the side of me, and this is a totally different sensation (*in the chest*) than I felt with them [the fishes] ... Yeah, I can feel them and the earth ...

JACK. What is the combination like?

CYNDY. I've never felt anything like it. I'm entirely open in a way I've never been before ... like experiencing the earth and the ocean and the sun all at once and totally.

JACK. You've opened up the emotional center in this dream; the life center in the first one. That's beyond my expectations. I wonder, with these two centers open, have you had a dream about your head since then?

CYNDY. How would I know that a dream is about my head or not?

JACK. Well, you would feel it there. You would have something about energy or power in your head.

CYNDY. No, I don't think so ... I had this dream — I don't want to work on it. I worked on it with my trainees, one day they didn't have anything to work on and they wanted to practice ... I had remembered a vision, a dream, or a daydream ... a frame, a picture frame, and I got into this place of feeling all this energy ... like that first dream ... I don't know how to describe it, just feeling so much ... like a secret place I found ... and in order to get into this place, it was on a beach, I went through these rocks with a hole in it to find my way through ... I literally in the group felt like a dolphin, like a fish, and moved totally alone and at peace with myself. I was on my back feeling all this energy. Then I experienced this figure over me, a gray cloud in the form of a human. I could feel the energy, I reached my hands up and felt the energy coming down my arms into my body. I felt this strong red energy moving into the left side of my body ... but I don't know what it meant ... I felt the energy for two hours ...

<175>

JACK. Perhaps we could work further sometime. Let's stop here, OK?

CYNDY. Yeah ... I feel more complete, finished.

COMMENTARY

Cyndy has moved into areas of experience uncommon to our contemporary cultural space-time structure. They are more common to other cultures where study groups could be maintained over many centuries — in Tibet, and among the Sufis of Central Asia, and the Hindus of India.

Spontaneous opening of the life and emotional centers occurs in our own culture to a limited extent. In the worship of the Sacred Heart of Jesus and the saying of the Rosary we have methods for realizing the emotional center. In our athletic and military organizations we have crude yet effective methods for developing and utilizing the belly or life center. Unfortunately, the life center in our culture is completely amoral; it is solely concerned with survival and reproduction. The history of military organizations around the world shows that the tragic record of the American military in Vietnam is in no way unique. Divorcing life-center activities from the other three centers (emotional, intellectual and spiritual) leads to horror.

The object of human development beyond basic survival is the harmonious integration of all four centers — the life center, the emotional center, the intellectual center, and the spiritual center — into total consciousness. A conscious awareness that recognizes and experiences our human uniqueness as inseparable from all life, all awareness, all being.

Cyndy is open to the astounding variety of life experiences available to those who have sufficiently cleansed themselves of the hindrances and hangups of our technological civilization. She is experiencing life more abundantly than most of us; the life within

<176>

herself, the life all around her, and, yes, even the life beyond this level of experience we call "here and now."

> ... The gloom of the world is but a shadow —
> Behind it, yet within our reach, is Joy —
> There is radiance and glory in the darkness
> could we but see, and to see we have only
> to look — I beseech you to look —
> And so at this time I greet you —
> Not quite as the world sends greetings,
> but with profound esteem and with prayer
> that for you now and forever the day breaks,
> and the shadows flee away—

> — Fra Giovanni, A.D. 1513

<177>

Join the Gestalt Journal Press On-Line Book Club

Send your email address to <club@gestalt.org> with "join" as the subject and receive a special promotion code that will give you a 15% discount at the online store with the most comprehensive selection of books, CDs, & DVDs relating to the theory and practice of Gestalt therapy available anywhere.
www.gjpstore.com

Explore the world of Gestalt therapy online and locate a Gestalt therapist in the International Guide to Gestalt Practitioners at
www.gestalttherapy.net

For a complete, up-to-date calendar of Gestalt therapy workshops, training events and conferences read *Gestalt News and Notes*
at
www.gestalt.org/news